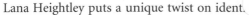

Lana Heightley puts a unique twist on ident.
as she attributes a gift to each of the women of the Bible whom sie
discusses. (Have you ever thought of Lydia exercising her gift of
administration?)

She also emphasizes the importance of recognizing and using our
gifts in ministry, especially as we serve with other women. From her
broad experience leading ministry teams of women overseas, Lana
describes how a well-balanced team functions as one body when the
motivational gifts are in place and how easily the relationships can
become dysfunctional when the gifts are not recognized or are misused.

—LORRY LUTZ
AUTHOR OF *WOMEN AS RISK-TAKERS FOR GOD* AND
LOOKING FORWARD TO THE REST OF YOUR LIFE?

Lana Heightley has broken a spiritual barrier for both women and
men. Every pastor should read this and better understand, from a
practitioner's insight, how to release the majority of their congregation into productive ministry.

Although Lana has chosen examples from women in the Bible,
she has also given practical illustrations from her vast experience
gained through years of leading teams overseas in ministry. She
shows how the various spiritual gifts complement one another and
strengthen the effectiveness of any team ministry. These same principles are vital across the board for both men and women serving in
the body of Christ. This is not theory—it works!

—DR. NAOMI DOWDY
SENIOR PASTOR, TRINITY CHRISTIAN CENTRE
SINGAPORE

Drawing from the lives of women in the Bible, as well as modern-day
women in ministry, Lana Heightley's book provides a foundational
teaching for women who want to discover and understand their
motivational gifts. She uses real-life examples to illustrate both the
blessings and the challenges that can occur when those with differing
gifts interact in the body of Christ. If you have been seeking to grow
personally and spiritually in understanding your motivational gift,
this book will be an encouragement for you!

—JANE HANSEN
PRESIDENT, AGLOW INTERNATIONAL

Filled with astonishing truths, Lana's book deeply challenges seasoned and new Christians alike. Highly recommended!

—BEVERLY LEWIS
AUTHOR OF *THE COVENANT AND SANCTUARY*

Presents From on High is a practical book written for women who desire to be in the ministry. Heightley has encouraged women of all walks of life to find their motivational gifts to serve the Lord and people. Women have been freed to use their talents. She illustrates her thesis by examples of women in the Bible: Mary, Martha, the woman at the well, and others. Women are freed from guilt, condemnation, and competition. It makes for balance in life situations and teamwork in ministry. This book belongs in the pastor's library as well as the women's guild. This is a must read—highly recommended.

—STANFORD E. LINZEY, JR., D.D., D.MIN.
AUTHOR OF *THE HOLY SPIRIT IN THE THIRD MILLENNIUM*

If you are a believer, you have at least one God-given gift. Discovering, developing, and using this gift is absolutely essential if you are to fulfill your divine destiny. How do you do this? Lana Heightley's book will guide you through this exciting journey.

—C. PETER WAGNER
CHANCELLOR, WAGNER LEADERSHIP INSTITUTE

Lana's experience leading teams is vast, varied, and valuable. Her understanding of gifting and how it affects teamwork has changed the way I do missions, counsel, and lead others. Her fresh approach to women in the Bible has encouraged women around the world to find their place in loving service.

—DR. MELONIE JANET MANGUM
ASSOCIATE PASTOR, MALIBU VINEYARD

Having worked with women in ministry both in the U.S. and overseas, I understand the unique challenge of blending different personalities into a dynamic ministry team. *Presents From on High* uses the gifts of the Spirit to explain the personality differences that are inevitable in any group effort, and gives practical, biblically sound ways to turn those differences into spiritual positives. Anyone working with women in ministry will benefit from reading this book!

—MARILEE PIERCE DUNKER
WORLD VISION CHILD SPONSORSHIP ADVOCATE AND
DAUGHTER OF WV FOUNDER, BOB PIERCE

PRESENTS FROM ON HIGH

LANA HEIGHTLEY

Charisma
HOUSE
A STRANG COMPANY

Most Strang Communications/Charisma House/Siloam products are available at special quantity discounts for bulk purchase for sales promotions, premiums, fund-raising, and educational needs. For details, write Strang Communications/Charisma House/Siloam, 600 Rinehart Road, Lake Mary, Florida 32746, or telephone (407) 333-0600.

Presents From on High
by Lana Heightley
Published by Charisma House
A Strang Company
600 Rinehart Road
Lake Mary, Florida 32746
www.charismahouse.com

Unless otherwise noted, all Scripture quotations are from the Holy Bible, New International Version. Copyright ©1973, 1978, 1984, International Bible Society. Used by permission.

Scripture quotations marked AMP are from the Amplified Bible. Old Testament copyright © 1965, 1987 by the Zondervan Corporation. The Amplified New Testament copyright © 1954, 1958, 1987 by the Lockman Foundation. Used by permission.

Scripture quotations marked KJV are from the King James Version of the Bible.

Scripture quotations marked NLT are from the Holy Bible, New Living Translation, copyright © 1996. Used by permission of Tyndale House Publishers, Inc., Wheaton, IL 60189. All rights reserved.

An effort has been made to locate sources and obtain permission where necessary for quotations used in this book. In the event of any unintentional omission, modifications will be gladly incorporated in the future editions.

Cover design by Terry Clifton

Library of Congress Control Number: 2003115716
International Standard Book Number: 1-59185-462-8

05 06 07 08 09 — 9 8 7 6 5 4 3 2
Printed in the United States of America

TO JOHN:

You have clearly lived up to 1 Peter 3:7: "In the same
way, you husbands must give honor to your wives. Treat
her with understanding as you live together" (NLT).
Without you this book would never have happened.
I am so blessed to have you as my husband.

ACKNOWLEDGMENTS

It is impossible to thank all those who have poured themselves into my life, helping to make me who I am today. How can I possibly name and thank all those who have loved me through the years and contributed to my spiritual development? To you I owe the greatest debt of thanks.

A few of those individuals must be recognized here for their direct and unique part in making this book possible.

- ❖ I will forever be grateful to my mother, Lagonia Lemons, who was my first mentor and spiritual mother. Words could never tell of my great love and gratitude for her. Next to Jesus, she will be the first one I will look for in heaven.

- ❖ My love for missions came from my father, Les Lemons. Thank you for believing that one is never too old to work for our Savior. Thank you for becoming a lay missionary at the age of sixty-nine.

- ❖ Powell Lemons, my faithful brother, pastor, trainer, and mentor for short-term missions, you taught me how to do it. I rejoice that you have now reached one million people for our Lord during your missions work. Thank you for being all that I needed and more in a brother.

❖ The many women who have been a part of Women With A Mission teams, each one of you is a gift from the Father. As we have traveled the world together in ministry, we have shared insights about God, laughed, cried, faced dangerous and difficult circumstances, and powerfully proclaimed the kingdom of God. The Father truly has partnered me with the best! A special thanks to all of you who have ministered with me.

❖ Marilyn (Lyn) Brown—Your stories are a valuable part of this book.

❖ Pastor Ted and Gayle Haggard, who mentor me every Sunday morning, you are true examples of those who model how to free people to operate in their gifts.

❖ Mary Busha, editor and publishing agent, you made my dream come true. Without your continual encouragement this book would have been in the circular file long ago. Thank you for being my friend and sage.

❖ Karen Roberts, thank you for your editing expertise and professionalism. You are truly amazing.

❖ The hundreds of intercessors who have prayed for this book, thank you for persevering.

❖ Most of all, best of all, thank You, Lord Jesus, for allowing me to partner with You for Your harvest. It is my highest calling.

CONTENTS

FOREWORD

My first introduction to Lana Heightley was during my early years as director of women's ministry at our church when she came and offered to help. We were launching women's small groups at that time, and she offered to open her home to women in her neighborhood and to lead them in a Bible study. Most of the women who attended her study were unchurched, and it was exciting to hear reports throughout the year of different ones meeting Jesus and being born again. Now six years later this group is still meeting regularly, growing in relationship with the Lord and with each other and leading more women to Jesus.

Lana has gone on to leading other small groups in the church from prayer and Bible study groups to teaching younger women homemaking skills such as quilting and cooking. In the midst of her service, I discovered she was also leading women's ministry teams around the world through her organization, Women With A Mission. Because of all her service to the local church and the body of Christ around the world, it is easy to conclude that Lana knows something about ministry, and she knows something about helping ministry teams work together to provide an effective service to the body.

According to the Scripture, each of us has gifts that are given to us to help the body of Christ function smoothly and effectively in fulfilling our purpose in the world. In this book, Lana helps us understand how our gifts function together and complement each other so we all benefit from what each person brings to the mix in team ministry. We all have gifts. Once we identify what they are, it is important that we don't keep them in an infant state by believing that our gift perspective is the only one of value. Rather, we must mature in our gifts and use them to strengthen the group. Then the whole body will benefit from the complimentary nature of our gifts, and we can enjoy the fellowship of ministering together.

Lana shows us how this all works as she shares her experiences and those of her ministry teams. This book will encourage the reader and help us all avoid unnecessary struggles as we endeavor to serve the Lord.

—GAYLE HAGGARD, NEW LIFE CHURCH
COLORADO SPRINGS, COLORADO

CHAPTER 1

THE SIGNIFICANCE OF MOTIVATIONAL GIFTS

Why in the world do we need another book about spiritual gifts? Authors such as Bill Gothard, C. Peter Wagner, Don and Katie Fortune, and others have already written many good books on this subject. In fact, I personally—as well as all the women who have served with me over the years on Women With A Mission teams— have greatly benefited from these books. The teachings in them helped us take the Good News of Jesus Christ to women around the world and raised them up to places of leadership through this ministry.

Although I have partnered with women in ministry in the United States and around the world since 1985, it wasn't until 1994 that our efforts were accomplished through a ministry I founded called Women With A Mission. Our mission is to affect our world for Christ by using the gifts He has given us to help others develop theirs. Many of our efforts involve teaching, training, and equipping women regarding their purpose and destiny in the Lord.

So, since there are good books on the topic of

motivational gifts, why am I offering yet another one? There are several reasons:

I have seen firsthand in women's ministry around the world how the motivational gifts listed in Romans 12:6–8—the gifts of perceiving, serving, teaching, encouraging, contributing, administration, and mercy— work together to build up and bring blessings to the body of Christ.

I have watched the proper use of these gifts bring unity and freedom, not only to the women who are using their gifts to minister, but also to the women who are receiving the fruit of these gifts.

I have witnessed the gifts being misused and misunderstood, resulting in disunity and division.

I am convinced that how we are motivationally gifted directly impacts how we respond to a variety of life situations and ministry opportunities.

I believe my ministry experiences and years of study of women of the Bible, combined with stories of modern-day women using their motivational gifts for the kingdom, add a unique and fresh perspective to what has already been written about spiritual gifts. Later in this chapter, I will tell the first of many stories recorded throughout this book that shows the motivational gifts at work among our Women With A Mission teams.

Primarily, I have written this book to help women determine their dominant motivational gift, understand its characteristics, and be challenged to use that gift to the fullest in individual, church-based, and women's team ministry. A secondary purpose for writing the book is to enable women to understand and appreciate other gifts and to encourage others to walk in them.

Finally, it is my desire that all women get to know the women of the Bible better. They are our first models of women in ministry, and their legacy to us is rich with understandings about how we can use our gifts in service and outreach.

In short, I believe *Presents From on High* will help women of all ages and all nations grow spiritually and personally as they experience new insights and challenges from key women of the Bible, as well as from modern-day women with similar motivational gifts.

You are about to discover in the pages of this book what so-called ordinary women of the Bible such as Martha of Bethany, Lydia the seller of purple cloth, and the woman at the well, to name a few, have in common with you and me. In the process, my desire is that you will discover your own unique motivational gifts and begin to walk freely in them.

God had a special work for each of the women of the Bible named in this book, and He has a special work for each one of us as we step out in faith, taking His message to our families, communities, and others around the world. Most important, He has already given each of us the gifts that enable us to do so.

WHERE DO YOU FIT INTO GOD'S PLAN?

You might ask, "How can I contribute to God's plan? Where do I fit in? How can I know His will for my life? What do I have to offer?" These are legitimate questions, all of which will be addressed in this book.

Clearly, your foremost calling as a Christian is to make disciples of all nations and to be a servant of God. (See Matthew 28:19 and Philippians 2:1–11.) However, to function most effectively, you must discover your *specific* place in the body of Christ and understand how you can best operate in it. (See 1 Peter 4:10.) You will find your unique place and means of ministry only by discovering, understanding, and operating in your spiritual gifts. When you do, your potential for ministry will be unleashed. You will be set free to walk in your gifts.

The core of our efforts in the Women With A Mission ministry is the belief that as women discover and function in their spiritual gifts they are led to their God-ordained placement in the body. The results? Women discover how to use their gifts in their callings, and they are empowered to do more together than they could on their own.

CALLING VS. GIFTS

At this point you might be wondering, *What is the difference between my spiritual gifts and my calling?* Basically, your *spiritual gifts* are God's investment in you, activated for Christian service when you invite Christ into your life. *Calling* is your passion and vision. So, your calling is how you implement your spiritual gifts. Let me say that another way: your spiritual gifts determine the way you respond to the world, and your calling is the place God has given you to use your gifts.

For example, you may have the spiritual gift of mercy. You also may have a passion to minister at homeless shelters. Your gift of mercy, therefore, is put to work in your calling to serve those who are homeless.

VARIOUS TYPES OF GIFTS

The Bible lists several categories of gifts that are given to believers. In the 1970s Bill Gothard divided these gifts into three categories. Three groupings of these gifts are (1) manifestation gifts, (2) ministry gifts, and (3) motivational gifts.[1]

The apostle Paul talks about the first grouping in 1 Corinthians 12, where he says, "Now about spiritual gifts, brothers, I do not want you to be ignorant.... There are different kinds of gifts, but the same Spirit. There are different kinds of service, but the same Lord. There are different kinds of working, but the same God works all of them in all men" (verses 1, 4–6). The gifts that fall into this category are the *manifestation gifts.*

In Ephesians 4:11–13, regarding *ministry gifts,* Paul states, "It was he [Jesus] who gave some to be apostles, some to be prophets, some to be evangelists, and some to be pastors and teachers, to prepare God's people for works of service...and become mature, attaining the whole measure of the fullness of Christ." These ministry gifts also are known as the *fivefold ministry,* which is given to church-government leaders, whose job is to equip the saints for spiritual service.

The seven motivational gifts are for the work of the ministry and are given to all believers for service and outreach.

The third major portion of Scripture related to gifts is found in Romans 12:6–8. "We have different gifts, according to the grace given us. If a man's gift is prophesying, let him use it in proportion to his faith. If it is serving, let him serve; if it is teaching, let him teach; if it is encouraging, let him encourage; if it is contributing to the needs of others, let him give generously; if it is leadership, let him govern diligently; if it is showing mercy, let him do it cheerfully." These gifts can be referred to as *motivational gifts.*

Of course, the three passages just cited are not an all-inclusive list of the many gifts mentioned throughout the Bible. The gifts of leadership, intercession, celibacy, martyrdom, and helps are a few of the others named. The actual number of gifts given to Christians by God is debatable; however, some Bible scholars believe it to be as high as thirty. Of course, it's not the number of gifts that is important, but what we do with what God has given.

FOR SERVICE AND OUTREACH

In this book we will focus our attention on the seven motivational gifts listed in Romans 12:6–8. I've listed them below with brief descriptions of each. Because various versions of the Bible name the gifts differently, I use the names I believe most clearly describe the motivational gifts and, I hope, best differentiate them from the other gift lists.

As you will see in the many examples used in this book, these gifts are exemplified in the way we perceive, react, and respond to any given situation or to a need that may be presented to us.

It is very important to understand that each gift has special significance in the body of Christ. Don and Katie Fortune write in *Discover Your God-Given Gifts* that God gave Katie a picture of where each gift might fit as it relates to the physical body.[2] I've included her insights along with the description of each gift.

Perceiving (also known as prophesying): Perceivers have a special ability to proclaim God's truth without compromise, and they are quick to discern spiritual issues. Perceivers also tend to be strong-willed. They are considered the "eyes" of the body.

Serving: Servers are gifted in their desire and abilities to be of practical service. They work to meet the needs of others, sometimes even at the expense of their own physical needs and well-being. They are considered the "hands" of the body.

Teaching: Teachers enjoy researching, learning, and instructing others. They emphasize accuracy. They love to learn and share their knowledge. Very often they see things as either black or white. They are considered the "mind" of the body.

Encouraging (also known as exhorting): Encouragers love to encourage people to be all they can be, counsel those in need, and see others mature spiritually. They tend to be quite verbal. They are considered the "mouth" of the body.

Contributing: Contributors want to help meet the needs of the ministry. They joyfully give either material items or financial resources, and they usually have a keen ability for business. They are considered the "arms" of the body.

Administration (also known as leading): Administrators have strong leadership qualities and are able to organize people to achieve a common task or goal. They are considered the "shoulders" of the body.

Mercy: Mercy givers have compassion for people who are suffering mentally, physically, or emotionally. They are long-suffering and love to meet the needs of those in distress. They are considered the "heart" of the body.

In the chapters that follow, you will see each of these gifts exemplified in the life of a woman of the Bible as well as in the lives of modern-day women. We will begin our study with Martha of Bethany, whose life illustrates the gift of service. Servers in the body of Christ are the easiest to identify because the manifestations of their gifts are quite practical and usually very visible to others, according to research by Don and Katie Fortune.[3] After servers we will look at mercy givers, who are the most numerous in the church. Is it any wonder that God has gifted more people with mercy than any other gift?

Next we will explore encouragers, those people who love to tell others what Christ has done for them and to encourage everyone to experience all God has for them. By that time in our study the interactions of the various gifts in ministry will have become evident, so as we study perceivers we also will examine gifts working together effectively in teams.

The less common, but equally imporant, gifts of administration and teaching will be explored in the next two chapters. Finally, we'll take a look at the most rarely observed gift—contributing. The book wraps up the chapter-by-chapter with a discussion of the use of motivational gifts in perfect harmony, as Christ intended.

GIFTS WORKING IN REAL LIFE

An example of how the gifts work together and how those with varying motivational gifts perceive situations differently presented itself on one of our Women With A Mission team trips to India.

It was a hot, muggy September day in southern India. The air-conditioning in the van was struggling to keep us cool. There were seven women from the United States in the van—five of the motivational gifts were represented. That day we all were like children, straining our necks to take in the sights.

We were fascinated by what we saw: Brahman bulls with painted horns, open-air fish markets, villages teeming with people, streets filled with all manner of animals, and a myriad of idols along the roadside. The traffic, a mix of cars, buses, motorcycles, oxen carts, and bicycles, was unlike anything most of us had ever experienced. Even the woman from Los Angeles, who was accustomed to heavy traffic, had white knuckles!

At one point, two of our women screamed as another vehicle came within inches of hitting our van. Our driver, however, took it all in stride and never flinched. As we swayed from side to side on the road, dodging traffic, we wondered how our Indian hostess could be sleeping so peacefully in the front seat. After a while, though, we all settled down with our own thoughts, and eventually it became quiet.

We were on the road to Palayamkottai, where we would conduct a two-day conference. En route there, we had to pass through Madurai, which is home to the ancient Meenakshi Temple complex. It is the largest Hindu temple in southern India. Housed within the complex are many buildings, each several stories high and literally covered with brightly colored, hand-carved idols of Hindu gods. We all knew this area would be a place of increased demonic activity and thus one of great spiritual darkness. What we didn't know was how we would react individually and as a team.

In the van, besides the driver and our hostess, were two women with the gift of perceiving, one administrator, one server, one with the gift of mercy, and two encouragers. As we approached Madurai, both perceivers simultaneously became agitated and started to pray. The rest of us said nothing, but their prayers became louder and more forceful. Spiritual warfare had begun in earnest for these women! After a few minutes, one of the perceivers asked the team leader, who is an encourager, "Can't you feel the spiritual oppression?"

Not wanting the women to become fearful, she replied, "Yes, I can, but I just don't respond to it like you do."

Clearly upset, the perceiver said, "What? Don't you get it?"

"Yes," replied the encourager, "I do. But I can rest because I know that you are interceding for us, and I feel safe."

While we continued to make our way through the city, the perceivers became even more troubled that none of the other team members were joining them in spiritual warfare. Tension filled the van. The mercy giver leaned over to the encourager and asked, "Are they OK? Are they mad at you? Is everything going to be OK with the group?"

From the back of the van, the administrator asked, "Can't we just turn left at the next corner and get out of here?"

The encourager sitting to the right of the administrator replied, "It will be OK. We'll be through this area soon."

The server in the group stated: "I have some water back here. Would anyone like a bottle of water?"

Now somewhat humorous, this example shows how we perceive, react, and respond to any given situation based on our motivational gifts. It also shows how, if not understood and appreciated, our varying gifts can cause misunderstandings and discomfort.

VARYING GIFTS BRING FULLNESS AND BALANCE

It's important to remember that God gives each of us different gifts in order to bring fullness and balance to the body of Christ. Because we all operate in our motivational gifts, and because the gifts color the way we see and react to life, we would do well to understand and respect our own gifts as well as those of others.

First Peter 4:10 tells us, "Each one should use whatever gift he has received to serve others, faithfully administering God's grace in its various forms." Examining, then, what these motivational gifts are, and determining how to discover your own gifts and how they manifest themselves in various situations—some positive and some not so positive—is the purpose of this book.

The apostle Paul told the people of his generation not to be ignorant of their gifts. Similarly, you don't want to be ignorant of your gifts either. God is powerfully using women like you and me to serve His body and take His message of love to our families and neighborhoods and around the world. You can do that more effectively if you know and appreciate the gifts God has given you.

VARYING GIFTS BRING FREEDOM

In addition to fullness and balance, varying gifts bring freedom. Personally, discovering my own gifts set me free from self-condemnation, guilt, competition, and coveting other people's gifts. My own gifts are encouraging, teaching, and administration—the latter being my dominant motivational gift. Discovering my gifts has allowed me to operate in ministry using those gifts and not feel guilty that I'm not strong in areas where others are gifted. I am able now to operate more fully in my gifts and be content as others operate freely in theirs.

God desires that you be free to minister in whatever gift or gifts He has given you.

Let me say a word here about multiple and dominant gifts. I believe God has given each of us one or more motivational gifts. If we have been given only one, that gift makes us single-minded in its use. If we have been given many, we can feel pulled by varying urges and emotions. Understanding our dominant gift and its interaction with other gifts, whether in us or in others, is crucial to fullness and balance in ministry.

God desires that you be free to minister in whatever gift or gifts He has given you. By doing so, you embrace who you are in Christ and your own significance and uniqueness, which is your personal spiritual DNA. When you earnestly seek understanding, you will find your destiny and purpose in Christ. Secure in the role God has for you, you will be empowered with joy to operate in your own gifts and to celebrate with others whose gifts are different from yours. Perseverance and commitment to your calling will be established while you continue along your unique path of ministry, and you will be increasingly equipped to minister in the present-day move of God!

You and I, then, can rightly line up in that great army spoken of in Psalm 68:11 (AMP): "The Lord gives the word [of power]; the women who bear and publish [the news] are a great host." Wouldn't you like to be positioned exactly where God has destined you to be for winning your family, city, country, and other nations for the Lord?

We are living in unprecedented times! The world as we know it is changing so rapidly it is difficult to keep up. Daily we see on one hand nations and businesses failing; yet on the other hand we see the Spirit of God miraculously opening up families, cities, and nations to the knowledge of the Good News of Jesus Christ. His kingdom is being advanced!

Many Bible scholars today believe that we are living in a generation in which it is possible for every ethnic group to hear and learn the message of Christ. What a wonderful time to be alive. How exciting for those of us who have a passion for the lost souls of the nations and for those wanting to see the gospel of Christ furthered around the world. Truly, the window for affecting our world for Christ is wide open.

So let us cast into the deep. (See Luke 5:4, 6.) We are in this life together. The harvest is waiting to be shared.

When your opportunity comes, move freely in your gifts and be empowered for service and ministry!

For Further Thought

A motivational-gift assessment test appears at the back of this book. If you are uncertain about your dominant motivational gift, I encourage you to take a few moments to complete the test. Even if you already know your motivational gifts, taking the test may offer you new insights. I believe no matter where you are in your understanding that taking the test will enhance your reading of this book.

CHAPTER 2

LITTLE IS MUCH WHEN GOD IS IN IT:
Martha of Bethany

Martha of Bethany, the sister of Lazarus and Mary, enjoyed one of the greatest honors a woman could ever experience. She was a personal friend of our Lord Jesus Christ. This woman was loved by our Lord, and she demonstrated her love for Him in the practical ways women know how to do well—caring for Him in her home.

Martha's name appears twelve times in the New Testament, two of those times involving one-on-one dialogue with Jesus. She was deemed important enough to the Lord and His ministry that the writers of Luke and John both recorded stories of her encounters with Jesus as part of the permanent record of Jesus' life.

In recent history, however, this woman who served our Lord and was described by the apostle John as one loved by Jesus has mostly gotten a bad rap! Often she has been projected in a negative light by those who insinuate that she had a lousy attitude, that she had the audacity to question the Lord, that she was short-tempered and impatient, and that she had a penchant for making wrong choices. Her shortcomings are so visible in the accounts of her interactions with Jesus that her faith and gift of serving are rarely proclaimed.

Scripture offers us many insights into this amazing woman and the motivational gift that she used to contribute to Christ's ministry. Next to the gift of mercy, which all Christians are instructed by Jesus to extend toward one another, the gift of serving is the most commonly exercised and readily recognized motivational gift. Those who possess this gift are the "hands" of the body of Christ in the world.

A WOMAN OF FAITH

Perhaps the most well-known account of Martha's encounters with Jesus—and proof of their close friendship—is found in John 11. It is the story surrounding the death of Martha's brother, Lazarus, also a close friend of Jesus. Lazarus had become sick, so his sisters, Martha and Mary, sent word for Jesus, asking Him to come. They knew of His great love for Lazarus, and they were expectant that Jesus would help their brother.

Jesus delayed His coming, however, not arriving until four days after Lazarus's death. Because many Jews believed that a person's soul would linger nearby for three days while waiting to reenter the body, the significance of the four days is important to what occurred next.[1] Because three days had elapsed, Martha, among others, was certain there was no hope for Lazarus to live again.

As Jesus approached the outskirts of Bethany, Martha was the first to run to meet Him. She said, "Lord,…if you had been here, my brother would not have died. But I know that even now God will give you whatever you ask" (John 11:21–22). The urgency of the hour was in her voice. She expressed her frustration and anger as well as a litany of pain. In essence she was asking, "What was so important that You delayed Your coming? Don't You care about our great loss?" Certainly there was no trepidation on her part when it came to confronting Jesus with her feelings and thoughts. And clearly she knew Him sufficiently well to point out His character and His relationship with the Father of life.

Her final statement in this passage indicates her confidence in His power to do something in spite of the number of days that had passed since her brother's death. Martha was unafraid to express her hurt and sorrow along with her faith, for she knew that Christ's presence and power could have altered the situation had He only come in time.

After Jesus told her that her brother will live again, Martha instantly agreed and expressed her faith that indeed someday Lazarus would be resurrected. Here, perhaps because of her bold statement of faith, Jesus captured a moment in history that revealed a foundational tenet of our faith. He rewarded her faith with hope when He said, "I am the resurrection and the life. He who believes in me will live, even though he dies; and whoever lives and believes in me will never die" (John 11:25–26). This is the blessed hope of eternal life we all can embrace in our times of loss. Because He lives, we too will live.

MARTHA THE SERVER

The account of Martha that has raised so much disdain in modern history begins in Luke 10 with Jesus making one of His visits to her home in the little village of Bethany, located on the southwestern slope of the Mount of Olives, about two miles from Jerusalem. There Martha resided with Lazarus and Mary, the three siblings whom the apostle John says Jesus loved. (See John 11:5.) Martha obviously kept a home that was welcoming to visitors and had a sense of peace. According to Scripture, Jesus stayed there often. Perhaps there He felt He could unwind and rest with these friends who were like His own earthly family.

On this occasion, Jesus, along with twelve of His friends, shows up at the home of Martha, Mary, and Lazarus. "As Jesus and his disciples were on their way, he came to a village where a woman named Martha opened her home to him" (Luke 10:38). Typical of Jesus, He had just completed a long, tiring day of teaching and training.

After walking the hot, dusty road from Jerusalem to Bethany, Jesus and His disciples were no doubt looking forward to a nice evening of rest and a good meal. Whether or not Martha expected them is uncertain, but it appears that she did not. Can you imagine having thirteen or more unexpected guests drop in for dinner? Whatever the reason or circumstance surrounding her guests' visit, Martha proceeded to prepare a meal for them.

Now let's read what happens next.

> [Martha] had a sister called Mary, who sat at the Lord's feet listening to what he said. But Martha was distracted by all the preparations that had

to be made. She came to him and asked, "Lord, don't you care that my sister has left me to do the work by myself? Tell her to help me!"

"Martha, Martha," the Lord answered, "you are worried and upset about many things, but only one thing is needed. Mary has chosen what is better, and it will not be taken away from her."

—LUKE 10:39–42

Before looking further at the story, it is interesting to note that scholars believe Martha was the eldest in the family and that she most probably embodied what sociologists today call the *first-born syndrome*.[2] These people are typically self-sufficient, bold, and independent.

In the Jewish culture, being the eldest female in the family added the burden of being required to meet all the hospitality needs of the family's guests. Consequently, Martha was obligated to serve, and on this occasion she had to make do with what was in her cupboard. The markets were open only in the mornings, so they were long since closed for the day. Linda Rios Brook, a teacher and speaker, humorously notes, "Pizza Hut did not deliver in Bethany."[3]

Notice that as Martha worked to prepare a meal for the Lord and the twelve other guests, her sister, Mary, placed herself at the feet of Jesus, "listening to what he said." For several reasons, Martha showed alarm. First, her younger sister was sitting at the feet of Jesus, which was a position of learning. In those days women were not taught as men were. Learning in that way was culturally off-limits to women. Second, Martha was distressed because her sister was making no attempt to help her prepare the meal and serve their guests. Do you think Martha had reasons to be upset? I do.

Perhaps she was embarrassed by her sister's behavior. Undoubtedly she felt pressure, and she must have been just plain irritated over the whole situation. Martha was offended, and she probably felt like she was being taken advantage of. She was miffed, and she didn't hesitate to show it.

In this story, something becomes quite clear about Martha. She exhibited all the traits of a woman who had the motivational gift of serving.

WHAT ARE SERVERS LIKE?

It's easy to spot those who have the gift of serving. First, they just automatically provide for the needs of others. They are quick to see needs and quick to respond. They are hands-on people. And, because hospitality is an integral part of the gift of serving, servers often open their homes to others or find themselves in charge of events at church or elsewhere that require the preparation and serving of meals and seeing to the needs of guests.

> *It's easy to spot those who have the gift of serving. First, they just automatically provide for the needs of others.*

Servers are practical and down-to-earth, and they often go to any length to minister to others. They enjoy contributing to the overall success of some event or activity. Their contributions are often invaluable. They work hard to meet the practical needs of others and sometimes they wonder why others don't see the needs and join in to help meet them.

Many of these characteristics of servers are apparent in Martha. Did you notice that she didn't hesitate to bring Jesus and His friends into her home when they arrived? It was obvious to her that Jesus was tired and hungry, so she went right to work getting a meal ready. Martha was most definitely a practical person, a fact made obvious when she took it upon herself to minister to the practical needs of Christ and His friends. She certainly showed she was down-to-earth by suggesting that Jesus tell Mary to give her a hand in the kitchen. The need was so obvious—so why didn't others see it and join her in the preparations? She too may have wanted time with Jesus, but she chose to give the practical needs of the moment priority over her own needs.

SERVERS ARE EVERYWHERE

We all know people with the gift of serving. Our churches overflow with them. Mostly they are the *doers* in the church, the ones we can count on to help get the job done. And the jobs are endless: planning and preparing church dinners, running the sound board, setting up rooms for meetings, helping in the nursery, doing custodial work, serving the pastoral staff, to name just a few.

According to Don and Katie Fortune in their book *Discover Your God-Given Gifts*, about 17 percent of the people in the church have the gift of serving.[4] Quite literally, servers are the "hands" in the body of Christ (Prov.

31:20, AMP). Servers are the ones who answer many of the world's felt needs.

MODERN-DAY MARTHAS

Several years ago, I was a leader in Aglow International. During that time a woman named Rhonda attended our monthly meetings, where we enjoyed potluck lunches. It was Rhonda's responsibility to set up our tables and see to all the needs in the kitchen. Rhonda loved gracing our tables with beautiful flowers from her well-tended garden. Her banquet-table settings were truly a sight to behold. She was faithful to serve us every month.

After a while, however, our board of directors decided that the lunches had become impractical, and we eliminated them. Shortly thereafter, Rhonda stopped coming to our meetings. We didn't realize it at first, but later some of us concluded that by discontinuing our lunches we had inadvertently taken away Rhonda's ministry! Apparently, she no longer felt needed or valued by our group.

When we recognized what had happened, our board then decided to have a refreshment time before each of our meetings, and Rhonda returned. Once again, with her gift of serving, she could feel like she was contributing to the overall success of our gatherings.

I can imagine that Martha of Bethany must have experienced some of the same feelings Rhonda experienced. Like Rhonda, she was prompted by her motivational gift of serving to automatically want to meet the practical needs of her guests (and she would have appreciated a little help from her sister). When she asked for help and did not receive it, she probably wondered if Jesus—or anyone else—even realized or cared that her contribution was essential.

I know firsthand, and you probably do too, how both Rhonda and Martha must have felt. Although I do not score all that high in the gift of serving, from time to time this gift kicks in. Numerous times I have worked feverishly preparing for an event while others stood around, seemingly doing nothing to help. This is when I remind myself we all have different gifts and that my service is to the Lord.

Perhaps now you can see more clearly why the server in chapter 1, in our van story in India, reacted the way she did to the situation. At the peak of tension, her response was to meet needs in the most practical way she could: "I have some water back here. Would anyone like a bottle of water?" In fact, her offer of water was just what some of the women needed.

Another example of one of our team members using her gift of serving occurred on one of our ministry trips to the island of Borneo. Those of us from the United States who made up the Women With A Mission team were joined on this trip at a Malaysian airport by Pastor Nora from the Philippines. Though Nora had always been with us at our conferences for the Filipino women, this was the first time she had joined our American team outside of her own country.

As the team got off the plane and headed for the baggage claim area, everyone gathered around Nora, greeting her and expressing pleasure that she would be joining our ministry team in Malaysia. Another encourager and I were looking forward to having this special woman room with us.

One morning, about four days into our trip, we awoke to find Nora on her knees in the bathroom. At first we thought she was praying in the "other" room so she wouldn't wake us. But soon we saw that she was scrubbing the floor. Later we saw her examining all the knobs and buttons on the toilet. It was quite different from the toilets she was used to in the Philippines. I think this was fascinating to Nora, but puzzling. She had figured out all but one handle on the right side of the toilet.

"What is this for?" she asked. Soon we heard her screech as water poured out of the *bidet* and flooded the entire bathroom. All three of us laughed, before joining efforts to sop up the water.

Nora pastors more than five hundred people in her church that ministers primarily to the poor in her area, but her position didn't prevent her from using her gift of serving to keep our room tidy and livable, an incredible accomplishment because we who are encouragers minister much better than we clean.

CHALLENGES FOR SERVERS

Operating freely in our gifts requires a finely tuned sense of balance. Those with the gift of serving sometimes, like Martha, get off focus and have to be reminded of the other matters at hand besides the immediate and practical needs. Too often, those with the gift of serving will expend their energy almost to the point of exhaustion in order to meet a need, frequently at the expense of themselves and their families.

I love Jesus' response to Martha when she came to

Him expressing her feelings about the workload and her sister's lack of participation in the kitchen. "Martha," He said, "you are worried and upset about many things, but only one thing is needed." Now this really speaks to me. I love to entertain and have guests in our home for dinner. I delight in preparing a beautiful table with gourmet cooking and all the trimmings. Matching tablecloth and napkins are a must, and the soup, salad, entrée, and dessert dishes are uniformly patterned.

A typical meal starts with homemade soup, followed by a salad that complements the entrée. I often use a sorbet at this point to clean the palate, and then I serve an entrée that took hours to prepare. The finale has to be an award-winning dessert accompanied by a specially selected coffee.

Although it is absolutely essential, critical, and necessary to wait on the Lord in order to hear His voice, there are also times when we are compelled to do something.

Needless to say, all of this effort is costly and takes hours—sometimes days—to prepare. I am exhausted by the end of it all. Even though I am contented in my exhaustion, my husband, John, often reminds me that our friends come mainly for the fellowship and that they probably would enjoy a simple, one-dish meal just as well.

Could it be that Jesus was saying something similar to Martha? That she did not have to prepare five elaborate dishes for her guests; that one would have been sufficient? Perhaps fellowship with Martha and her siblings and rest from the day was what Jesus needed most. Martha, in her desire to meet His practical needs, missed the deeper, spiritual needs. The tendency to be perfectionists and do more than they are asked to do is consistent with servers. Had Martha kept it simple, she, like her sister Mary, may have had time to sit at Jesus' feet and enjoy fellowship with Him.

One of my favorite sayings related to the gift of serving comes from nineteenth century poet Elizabeth Barrett Browning: "Earth's crammed with heaven, and every common bush aflame with God; but only those who see take off their shoes. The rest sit around it and pluck blackberries."[5]

Some teachers who expound on Martha's encounter with Jesus say that all Martha needed to do was sit at Jesus' feet. Then, like Mary, she would have chosen the better thing. But think about it: Martha, just like you and I, responded to Jesus' coming to her door according to her motivational gift. That is the main premise for this book. How we react and respond to situations in life is determined by how we are motivationally gifted. It would not have been natural for Martha to welcome Jesus into her home and only sit at His feet, neglecting His needs. Jesus, in turn, came to her because He knew she would serve Him faithfully according to her gift. Her flaw, I'm convinced, was one of balance only.

For a moment, let's consider that perhaps Martha's gift of serving got in her way momentarily, causing her to miss Jesus' timing. Although it is absolutely essential, critical, and necessary to wait on the Lord in order to hear

His voice, there are also times when we are compelled to do something. James, Jesus' brother, has written us a letter about being hearers *and* doers of the word. (See James 1:22.) We cannot be hearers only or doers only. Faith without works is dead. (See James 2:17.) To get it right, however, takes balance.

We know there's a time for worship and a time for serving. Tommy Tenney, author and speaker, once said that Martha entertained Jesus' humanity while Mary entertained His divinity.[6] Both were needed. Martha's gift of serving certainly is not inferior to Mary's gift. They are simply different. Both are given by God for the benefit of His church.

In John 12:2 we see Jesus once again visiting Martha's home. This time Scripture simply says, "Martha served." Perhaps no more details are offered here because her serving was in balance, appropriate for the occasion. Because servers remember others' favorite things and try to accommodate them, I'm sure she cooked Jesus' favorite food!

MARTHA'S LEGACY

Martha's encounters with Jesus are a wonderful legacy to us. She shows us much about faith, about relationships, and about serving others.

Her expressed faith in Jesus' character and power, in spite of the fact that her brother, Lazarus, had been dead for four days, is a powerful lesson for us about trusting God both *in* and *in spite of* all circumstances. Would we have been able to say the same?

The encounter in which Martha was busy serving the Lord while her sister sat at His feet shows us Martha knew exactly where to take her complaint. She said nothing to Mary but went straight to Jesus. That is another important lesson for us. Do you and I have that close of a relationship with Christ that we don't think twice about going to Him first with our problems rather than to our sisters in the church?

Finally, Martha of Bethany shows us the motivational gift of serving in action. Though her efforts were not perfectly in balance, she shows us how the gift compelled her to act. Much later, Peter's letter to Christians scattered throughout the region echoes Martha's example and Jesus' teaching about balance in service. Peter says, "Each one should use whatever gift he has received to serve others, faithfully administering God's grace in its various forms" (1 Pet. 4:10).

I believe that Martha experienced great joy in doing what was helpful. She was like all those with the gift of serving, who are constantly looking for ways to show their love for others in deeds and actions more than in words.

My prayer for each of us is that we "number our days aright, that we may gain a heart of wisdom" (Ps. 90:12). Remembering that some gifts are more visible and public than others, we can then acknowledge that all of the motivational gifts are equal, necessary in the body, and given by God for His purposes.

For Further Thought

1. If Jesus came to your door, how would your motivational gift cause you to respond?

_____

_____

_____

_____

2. If you have the gift of serving, describe a time when you were able to use your gift freely. How did others respond? How did you feel afterward?

_____

_____

_____

_____

3. Whatever your motivational gift is, describe a time when you wanted to use your gift but were stifled by someone or some circumstance. How did that make you feel?

_____

_____

_____

_____

_____

4. Name people you know who you believe have the gift of serving. What characteristics do you observe about them that show they have this gift?

_____

_____

_____

_____

CHAPTER 3

IN HIS TIME:
Mary, the Mother of Jesus

A rtists throughout the ages have painted her. Idols of her are everywhere. And each Christmas season we see her heralded as the humble, prayerful, obedient servant who delivers the Christ child. Mary the mother of Jesus, is the most famous and revered woman in all of history.

How could such a young girl, very possibly only fourteen years old at the time of Jesus' birth, merit such adulation down through the ages? Was it her courage and character alone, or was there more? Truly it was the desire of every young Jewish girl to give birth to the promised Messiah. Why, then, was Mary chosen and highly favored? What traits did this peasant girl embody that our heavenly Father would take notice of? What set her apart to deliver the Desired of all nations? (See Haggai 2:7; Daniel 11:37.)

Perhaps it was her attitude of total surrender, but possibly it was more—her lifelong capacity to love and show mercy. Why she was chosen and how she would choose to use her motivational gift of mercy may be one of the most important messages ever given to us by God.

A YOUNG GIRL'S STORY

We first see Mary in the Scriptures when she was approached by the angel Gabriel with the amazing news from God that she would bear the Christ child. How did this poor peasant girl from the hill country of Nazareth respond to the angel's message? She graciously and humbly accepted her position as the one to bring the Messiah into the world, taking no thought of her own reputation or the reputation of her family. She must have known that shame would have been the result of her obedience to the angel's announcement. Accepting this great call on her life certainly opened the possibility of losing Joseph, her betrothed. She must have known also that she would even risk death by stoning. (See Deuteronomy 22:20–24.) Yet she made the decision to be obedient and accepted the call on her life without hesitation. "I am the Lord's servant," Mary answered the angel Gabriel. "May it be to me as you have said" (Luke 1:38).

Though this young girl may have seen herself as small in her own eyes, her love for God was great. Her response shows that she didn't need to see the complete picture of what lay ahead in order to say yes. Luke 1:48 records her explanation to her cousin Elizabeth of the "why me" question any of us might have felt. Mary said simply, "For he has been mindful of the humble state of his servant."

While Mary was rejoicing with her cousin Elizabeth over Elizabeth's pregnancy, we catch a second glimpse of her character. Her love for God was beautifully demonstrated in her great song of praise, the Magnificat. (See Luke 1:46–55.) She adroitly glorified the Lord as her spirit rejoiced in Him and praised Him, because He had taken notice of the lowly. Mary expressed her reverential fear for Him and praised Him for lifting up the humble. She continued singing His praises by stating that He satisfies the hungry and is merciful to Abraham's descendants.

This young girl's song, filled with Scripture, also shows that she was a student of the Word. Notice her familiarity with Hannah's prayer, as her praise song is very similar. (See 1 Samuel 2:1–10.) Both women birthed the purposes of God: Mary, Jesus the Savior of the world; and Hannah, Samuel the great judge and prophet of whom it was said that none of his words fell to the ground and no one could find fault in him. (See 1 Samuel 3:19; 12:4–5.) Both women raised sons who found favor with God and with man.

MARY'S JOURNEY

As we look at various episodes in the life of Mary, from the time of Jesus' birth until long after His death, we see how she endured the difficult path ahead without complaint or resistance. Take a minute to imagine what was going on in Mary's mind when she and Joseph took Jesus to the temple to complete the law mandate for her purification. Upon presenting her Son, Jesus, to God, she encountered the old prophet Simeon who prophesied that Mary's soul would be pierced. Significantly, the Bible did not record a response from Mary. But from what we know of her character already, we can assume her response was once again one of humble acceptance.

True to this prophecy, there followed many occasions when Mary experienced extreme emotions and mental anxiety. One such occasion was recorded in Mark when the family of Jesus, embarrassed by His actions, commented that He was out of His mind. (See Mark 3:21.) How this remark must have hurt Mary, for she kept the events and promises of His birth and life in her heart. The Scripture recorded no response from her.

Another occasion for injury occurred when Mary was trying to get into the crowded room to hear Jesus. Jesus did not give her that special privilege. Instead, He asked, "Who are my mother and my brothers?" (Mark 3:33). Mary did not step forward to claim her status. Her response—or lack thereof—gave the generations that followed an example of how to handle the hurt of being unrecognized. After all, Mary remembered what God had spoken. She knew the Word. She had it hidden in her heart. She knew her value, even though it appeared that her Son had temporarily rejected her.

The greatest piercing of Mary's heart came at the Crucifixion. The suffering of Jesus must have been indescribable, and there was nothing this mother could do to alleviate it for Him or herself. Those dark hours between Calvary and Resurrection Sunday surely were the greatest heartbreak of all, but Mary remained faithful and took God at His Word. She waited, as she had all her life, to see God's promises to her fulfilled.

WHAT ARE MERCY GIVERS LIKE?

Of all the motivational gifts, the gift of mercy is the one with the greatest capacity to demonstrate love. Mercy givers are truly the "heart" of the body of Christ. They are the givers of compassion to a hurting world. How much does the world need mercy givers? One survey of gifting shows that 30 percent of all Christians have mercy as their dominant gift.[1]

Next to Jesus, Mary is the biblical figure who best demonstrated the gift of mercy in action. Jesus' first teacher was His mother Mary. She instilled her values in Him. What are the values of mercy evidenced in the lives of both Mary and Jesus?

Humility is one of the most obvious characteristics of mercy givers. We see several examples of humility in Mary as a young girl—her response to the angel Gabriel, her conversations with her cousin Elizabeth about being the one chosen to bear the Christ child, her many encounters with others when she showed that it was not she who was deserving of attention but Jesus.

Of all the motivational gifts, the gift of mercy is the one with the greatest capacity to demonstrate love.

Mary's humility is clearly shown in the account of the shepherds coming to visit the newly born Jesus, recounting their wondrous angelic visit. Mary did not try to outdo them by telling of her extraordinary visit by the angel Gabriel. We see her humility again when the Magi visited, telling of the star that led them to the house where Jesus was. Mary did not try to overshadow their joy by telling them of her own experiences. The Word simply says, "Mary treasured up all these things and pondered them in her heart" (Luke 2:19).

Jesus, of course, is our perfect example of humility. Scripture says that Jesus made himself of "no reputation" (Phil. 2:7, KJV). He was humble and willing to be a servant to all. He chose to eat meals with sinners and those regarded low in society. He washed His disciples' feet. He did not claim His rights as the Son of God when He stood before Pilate. These and other examples of Christ's humility are enough to fill the pages of many books!

Besides their humility, mercy givers most commonly manifest their gift through acts of compassion. Those with the gift of mercy have compassion for people who are suffering mentally, physically, or emotionally. They love to meet the needs of those in distress. An example of Mary's compassion is her response to the host at the wedding in Cana. (See John 2:1–11.) In all likelihood this was the wedding of John, her nephew—the man who was not only the disciple of Jesus, but may have been His cousin—John the Beloved. It was this John to whom Jesus later entrusted His mother's care at the Crucifixion. And it was he who gave us his eyewitness account of Jesus' life and ministry in the Gospel of John.

Mary's gift of mercy empowers her to endure her difficult path without complaint or resistance.

On this occasion Mary was concerned for the major social embarrassment of the bridegroom, and that concern led her to approach Jesus to plead for His help. Whether Jesus had previously performed miracles in

Mary's presence is not known, but she knew His character. She knew she could trust Him to do something in this situation. Her faith in her Son's abilities was great. Accordingly, her intercession for the bridegroom did not fall on deaf ears and Jesus honored His mother's request.

Scripture describes at least six occasions when Jesus was filled with compassion:

1. When He went throughout the villages and towns and noticed that the people were helpless because they didn't have a shepherd. (See Matthew 9:36.)

2. When He saw the sick and healed them. (See Matthew 14:14.)

3. When He fed the four thousand besides the women and children because they were hungry. (See Matthew 15:32–38.)

4. When He healed the two blind men at Jericho. (See Matthew 20:34.)

5. When He made whole the man who came to Him with leprosy. (See Mark 1:41–42.)

6. When He brought back to life the son of the widow of Nain. (See Luke 7:11–15.)

The gift of mercy is often characterized by the avoidance of conflict or confrontation. Mary did not argue with those who insulted her Son, saying He was crazy. She did not protest or claim her rights when she came to see Jesus and He used the occasion to ask the crowds, "Who are my mother and my brothers?" Instead, Mary's gift of mercy empowered her to endure her difficult path without complaint or resistance.

Jesus, too, was careful to avoid conflict, preferring the way of peace, but because He embodies all the gifts, He knew when to challenge the authorities. He avoided conflict in John 8:48–59 where, before the Jews, Jesus made the claim that He is God. When the Jews picked up the stones to stone Him, rather than confront them, Jesus slipped away from the temple grounds. However, when confrontation was necessary, driving out all who were improperly buying and selling in the temple, He was a man of action. (See Matthew 21:12–13.)

Mercy givers also are sensitive to the feelings of others, and they always look for the good in people. In addition, they search for opportunities to give preference or place to others by putting them first. We see Mary doing this very thing when she went to help Elizabeth. She went during the last three months of Elizabeth's pregnancy and the first few days after John's birth. Clearly, Mary was more interested in helping her relative than minding the issues of her own early pregnancy.

Mercy givers are humble, compassionate peacemakers. They put others above themselves. In so doing, their hearts transform the hearts of others.

A MODERN-DAY MARY

One of the greatest blessings our Women With A Mission teams experience is the opportunity to minister, serve a meal, and distribute clothing and shoes to lepers through the India Gospel League's outreach in Salem, India. Though virtually unknown to us, the disease of leprosy is still a major medical condition in India. The experience of ministering compassion to the lepers was an especially exciting one for our team in the year 2000. I have beautiful memories of the women graciously feeding these people, praying with them, playing with their babies, and handing out sandals as gifts.

Mercy givers often minister through loving action, and Sheila, one of our team members, demonstrated her mercy giving that day. Following our group's time of ministry, most of the team members headed back to our van for the journey back to the missions base. Sheila, however, stayed behind after the others began to regroup. When I went back to look for her, I found her kneeling at the feet of a young woman who had a baby in her arms. Both Sheila and the young mother had tears running down their faces as Sheila gently fastened the Velcro fasteners of the sandals over the woman's toeless feet. Then I noticed she also had no fingers. The specific need of this woman was not seen by the rest of us on the team, but Sheila, our mercy giver, was drawn to this young woman who needed help putting on her new sandals.

Compassionate acts are a lifestyle for Sheila. I recall another incident where her gift of mercy was vividly displayed. At this particular time in her life, Sheila was supervising an Aglow telephone hotline in her home. She received a call on Thanksgiving morning from a woman who was stranded in downtown Portland. She had no money or extra clothes, and she needed food and a bed for the night. Sheila and her husband, Wayne, drove downtown and brought her back to their home for Thanksgiving dinner and provided a bed for the night in a hotel. The following day, they helped her receive further assistance.

MINISTRY CHALLENGES FOR MERCY GIVERS

Some motivational gifts have a tendency for bringing about conflict, but mercy givers typically get along well with everyone. They avoid conflict. Sheila, for example, can room with anyone on missions trips with great joy and cheerfulness, and she rarely experiences or causes strife.

Mercy givers and those who work alongside them, however, do have challenges. Although this gift is much needed in the body of Christ because it reaches out to the hurting, there are downsides to watch for. Often mercy givers over-extend themselves at the expense of their, and others, well-being. Others are quick to notice, while the mercy givers seem oblivious to the potential problems of their actions. Fortunately, Sheila's delay after the leper gathering did not put her in any personal danger or greatly inconvenience our exhausted team, but on another occasion it might have.

Another challenge for mercy givers is their tendency to empathize too much with the suffering, which can take a heavy toll on them and others if not kept in balance. Helping to the detriment of one's own family, for example, can create financial and relationship problems within the family. Further, because mercy givers empathize so strongly with those who suffer, they can become enablers. That is, rather than teaching others to place their hope in the Lord, mercy givers can inadvertently cause others to become dependent on them.

In the case of Sheila bringing the woman into her home on Thanksgiving Day, the opportunity for overextending was present. If Sheila's husband had not readily agreed to this impromptu change of plans for their family holiday, the exercising of her motivational gift could have created conflict. Also, the danger of the woman taking advantage of Sheila's goodness or making herself dependent on Sheila's mercy was a distinct possibility on this occasion.

Mary's Gift of Mercy
in the Fullness of Time

In Ecclesiastes 3:1, Solomon said, "There is a time for everything, and a season for every activity under heaven." A look at the full life of Mary the mother of Jesus teaches more about her gift of mercy. It shows us how she graciously dealt with her changing roles as a woman and her gifting throughout the seasons of her life.

As a young woman, Mary valued her role of motherhood and its responsibilities. Her reaction to the initial separation as the caregiver of Jesus is noted in Luke 2:41–51. The occasion was the Feast of Passover, and Jesus was only twelve years old. After the feast and en route home, Mary and Joseph discovered that Jesus was not with them. Naturally they went back to Jerusalem to fetch Him.

Upon their arrival, Scripture tells us that they were astonished when they saw Him interacting with the teachers at the synagogue. (See Luke 2:48.) Mary reprimanded Jesus gently for causing them to be anxious. Notice His response to her about "being in my Father's house" (verse 49). Notice, too, that she accepted His statement. Mary recognized that her role was changing, and at that moment she graciously and humbly began the process of giving up control.

At the Cana wedding, Mary was in a place of service as a companion to her Son as His ministry unfolded. She knew that Jesus had the ability to help out. She saw that she, too, had something to contribute, for as a result of her plea to Jesus and His response by turning the water into wine, His earthly ministry was initiated. Although there was some discussion, it was Mary who saw the need and instructed those around her to "Do whatever he tells you" (John 2:5), and they did.

The episode of Mary being barred from the over-crowded room shows her continued release of her Son into His ministry. Mary understood the timing and the season of her life. In this instance, she refrained from asserting her rights. She recognized that her influence over her Son was waning.

At the cross, Mary experienced major life-changing events. Once again she entered into a new season and a new level of growth. Apparently she was widowed, her adult children were not followers of her Son whom she believed to be the Messiah, and Jesus experienced a hor-rible death at the hands of the Romans. At this point, she entered into a new relationship with the disciple John at the request of her Son—one of being John's mother and he her son. (See John 19:25–27.) John would now care for her, and she accepted his care for her. But, most impor-tantly, she lost her beloved Son. Jesus knew her gifting, and I like to think that He gave her a new adult son to minister to and with. She accepted His new direction for her life as humbly as she once accepted Gabriel's words about God's call on her life.

The last vignette we have of Mary is when she joined with the other disciples in the upper room to wait for the Holy Spirit. (See Acts 1:14.) Here is yet another transition for this gracious woman. She had now identified herself with others who would become known as the "church." She was present and praying with the others. Again she was found faithful. She was still following hard after God.

Timing is everything. Notice that even Jesus came in the fullness of time. (See Galatians 4:4.) Timing in our lives means actual chronological time, but it also relates to the right time for certain activities. I call this "right time" the *kairos* moment—the window of opportunity for precise activities. As Dutch Sheets states in his book *Intercessory Prayer*, "*Kairos* is the strategic or right time; the opportune point of time at which something should be done."[2]

A look at the natural seasons helps us see activities and opportunities that are appropriate for a lifetime of effectiveness. The early years of our lives can be compared to springtime when seeds are planted and nurtured, and they start to grow. In these times our character, strengths, and gifts are noticeable to others and us, but they must continue to be nurtured and practiced. Springtime is our time for maturing and preparation. Mary's springtime season extended from young motherhood to letting go of her Son to fulfill His adult ministry.

The summer season is a time for rapid growth and great production of fruit. Pastor and author Jack Hayford believes that between forty and sixty years of age is the time when first fruit begins to be harvested, the time when there's a new depth of understanding and effectiveness.[3] Ministries flourish during these years. This season was reflected in Mary when she worked alongside her Son in ministry and ministered to Him. It was also reflected in times with her sisters in the faith: Mary Magdalene; Mary, the mother of

James; Salome; Mary and Martha of Bethany; Joanna; Mary the mother of Clopas; and other friends. Mary and these women were willing to make commitments and take on responsibilities, and they remained faithful to complete their tasks. It was the time in their lives for action.

The autumn season is the one with the most vibrantly beautiful colors. I love this time of year. It is when I remember joyous times with family and friends in the past, and I begin my planning for the upcoming holidays. The coming of Mary into the upper room gathering can be called the beginning of her autumn season. Her passion for spiritual things had not decreased. Rather, it had increased! We see her anticipating the coming of the Holy Spirit, and she was prepared to tarry with the followers of Jesus as long as it took. She wanted all God had for her.

One year our Women With A Mission team ministering in the Philippine Islands was made up entirely of ladies in the autumn of their years. With the exception of one thirty-eight-year-old, the rest of us were between the ages of forty-five and sixty. Usually the teams are more diverse. What a surprise for the Filipino women who attended the conference where we spoke! They were of the mindset that anyone over forty was too old to be effective in the kingdom of God. Daily they commented on how wonderful it was to see grandmothers ministering for the Lord.

As a result of this trip, many of the team members and Filipino women went home and approached their own pastors about new areas of ministry. I regularly receive reports from these women, who are now much more actively partnering with their pastors in evangelism, prayer, and training. They have discovered that even in the autumn of their years they still have many opportunities for influencing people for the kingdom.

Every autumn John and I drive through the glorious mountains of Colorado. The sights of fall are truly breathtaking. They remind me of our lives. Like the resplendent trees breaking forth in all their glory, we, too, are going from glory to glory.

History tells us that Mary spent the winter years of her life with John the Beloved (her nephew) in Ephesus. The winter spiritual life is a time for roots to go deep. This is a time to prepare for the coming season of new life. It is a time for activities to be somewhat dormant so that new life can be produced. I believe Mary, like many older women I know, became a tremendous intercessor. I am confident her prayers for John were instrumental in his release from imprisonment on the Isle of Patmos.

In her winter years, Mary remained faithful. Her value was not based on activities but rather on who she was in the Lord. As Jack Hayford says, "Life's winter will finally claim my physical frame, but ahead for each of us whose faith is in Christ there is another springtime, the resurrection."[4] What a blessed hope!

THE FULLNESS OF TIME IN MY LIFE

In the summer of 1958, when I was fourteen years old, I went to a youth camp in the beautiful San Bernardino Mountains in southern California. Like all of my friends, I was passionate and full of zeal for the Lord. I was idealistic about life and believed God had a special plan for my life. All He had to do was show me what to do.

It happened on a Thursday night. The Lord gave me a vision, which ultimately was a call to the mission field. With every good intention, I responded, "Yes, Lord, here I am. Send me." Naturally I expected to go immediately.

I eventually married, had children, and busied myself with family. For many years this vision never came to fruition. I managed to live those years with a great deal of guilt and condemnation. Every time missionaries came to our church, my emotions ran the gamut from shame and failure, to feelings of outright rebellion. I had no understanding then that timing is everything with God. I was thinking I needed to be a missionary during my season of motherhood. Although this works for many women, it was not to be for me.

Following the principle "Do what your hands find to do," I started working in the church. Since my children were small, my ministry started by working in the nursery. I, then, went on to coordinate the nursery workers' schedule. As my children grew, I taught Sunday school classes, beginning with the third grade and graduating up to the adult class. In other words, as I was faithful to perform the small jobs right in front of my eyes, doors opened to more responsible ones. As the years passed, I prepared by studying God's Word, and I offered my services wherever I could. At the proper time, the Lord opened the doors for the unique missions work He had waiting for me.

My story is consistent with the story of the talents and the principle found in Luke 16:10–12, "Whoever can be trusted with very little can also be trusted with much, and whoever is dishonest with very little will also be dishonest with much. So if you have not been trust-worthy in handling worldly wealth, who will trust you with true riches? And if you have not been trustworthy with someone else's property, who will give you property of your own?"

MARY'S LEGACY

Mary's pilgrimage through life is a model for ours, regardless of our particular motivational gift. Perhaps this is one reason why she has continued to be revered down through the ages. We, like Mary, have heard God's promises to us; we are therefore called to take on an attitude of faith and not resistance. We choose to trust God in the dark times, just as Mary did, and we do what He places in front of us to do in every season of our lives.

The Scriptures challenge, "Who despises the day of small things?" (Zech. 4:10). Mary was faithful in the small things, and God the Father showed her favor by enlarging her influence in response to her obedience. You may think your life is small and insignificant, but God doesn't. His plan for a life of abundance for you was planned before the foundations of the world. "For we are God's workmanship, created in Christ Jesus to do good works, which God prepared in advance for us to do" (Eph. 2:10).

Proverbs 18:16 says a woman's gift makes a way for her. Are you allowing God to make a way for you rather than trying to place yourself in a position where the door has not yet opened? Maybe you find yourself chained to your past. Maybe you, like I did once, feel chained to the present.

Myles Monroe in his book *Seasons of Change* states, "Ignoring the season of change will forfeit destiny."[5] Let's search our hearts and make sure we are in the right season of our lives, chronologically as well as spiritually. Let's look at Mary's life as a legacy to find our place in ministry for all of life. Let's make the necessary paradigm shift. If we don't, we will find ourselves irrelevant in reaching this world for Christ.

Timing was everything for Mary, too. She brought Jesus physical life, and He brought her eternal life. In the fullness of time, Christ came to her. Too often we think that our lives will never change, or we see no real changes in our circumstances. But just as Jesus came to the world and to Mary's life at the right time, He, too, will enter into your world. Continue in faith believing in His trustworthiness, and be prepared to watch miracles happen.

Mary truly gave us an example of a life of excellence. She exercised her motivational gift of mercy faithfully all the days of her life. She graciously extended mercy and compassion to all around her, put her gift to work when Jesus needed her to, and understood the seasons of her life. In so doing, she literally brought forth God's purposes.

For Further Thought

1. Do you or does someone you know have the motivational gift of mercy? Describe a time when you recognized the gift of mercy in yourself or someone else.

_____

_____

_____

_____

_____

2. As He did for Mary the mother of Jesus, has God called you to do something that the world might not be able to understand? How have you answered God's call? What are the results?

_____

_____

_____

_____

_____

3. Is there a new area in your life in which God is asking you to be obedient? Explain.

_____

_____

_____

4. In what season of life are you? Describe what you are able to do, spiritually and chronologically, with your motivational gift because you are in this particular season.

_____

_____

_____

_____

_____

CHAPTER 4

GO TELL IT ON THE MOUNTAIN:
The Samaritan Woman

She was a woman of Sychar, but we know her best as the Samaritan woman or "the woman at the well." Most of us wouldn't consider her a gifted woman to be used in the kingdom of God. After all, she had been married five times and was living with a man who wasn't her husband. How could God use a woman like this to further His kingdom work?

The Samaritan woman's encounter with Jesus happened while she was going about life in her usual way, at a particular moment when she was going to draw water. (See John 4:3–42.) She had no idea she was about to meet the Messiah. She had no idea her life would be anything other than the collection of unsuccessful relationships it had been over her last several years. As she ran back to her village that day to tell everyone about this wonderful man she'd met named Jesus, her gift of encouragement was released for use in the kingdom.

A MOST UNUSUAL ENCOUNTER

Several aspects of this encounter were out of the ordinary. First, because each household needed for water to be brought to the home, her trip to the well was an everyday occurrence. From her little mountain village of Sychar on the eastern slope of Mount Ebal, she had traveled about a half mile down the road to the city well, the well that had been dug by Jacob and was part of the land Jacob had given to his son Joseph. To the people of that region, Jacob was their prophet and highly esteemed ancestor. His well, 138 feet deep, was part of the heritage of the Samaritans, who considered themselves Jacob's ancestry.

Why, however, had she chosen the heat of the day instead of the cool of the morning or evening to fetch water? Could her timing say something about her standing in society? Did she feel shame, hurt, rejection, humiliation, insecurity, or guilt? Perhaps she was proud, or perhaps she just wanted to be alone. Whatever her reason for going to the well at noon, she knew she most likely would not encounter others there at that time.

The second out-of-the-ordinary circumstance on this day was that a stranger had also come to the well at noontime. It was Jesus. He and His disciples had just completed a successful meeting and had baptized many people. Jesus was becoming more popular than John, who was known as the Baptist, and this popularity had stirred up jealousy among the religious officials. As a result, Jesus and His disciples had left town and headed north to Galilee.

Between Judea and Galilee was the political district of Samaria, considered by devout Jews as the home of the half-breeds. The Jews looked down on the Samaritans because they were descendants of mixed marriages between Israelites and Assyrians. (See 2 Kings 17:24–41.) No pureblooded, devout Jew would enter that area for fear of being contaminated, or made "unclean" according to Jewish regulations. Rather than going along the outskirts of Samaria and across the Jordan River, as was customary for Jews to do, Jesus instead took the shortest route and proceeded directly through Samaria. His group had probably left early in the morning, so they not only were tired but also hungry. Scripture says Jesus sent His disciples to buy lunch while He sat down by Jacob's well.

There at the well the unlikely encounter took place. The Samaritan woman and Jesus met face to face. She had approached to draw water; He to rest. They had nothing in common: not their gender, race, social status, education, or ethnicity. In fact, for more than seven hundred years there had been bitter rivalry between their two races. What made Jesus break the social taboo that day? More important, why did He speak to this person whom devout Jews called "a Samaritan dog"?

The fact that this stranger spoke to her certainly captured her attention. She was totally taken off guard by His request for a drink of water. Keenly aware of the social norm in this situation, she understood that this Jewish man was breaking all religious, social, gender, and cultural rules by being there and by speaking to her. And He'd asked her for a drink of water! Certainly He did not want to take a drink from her water pot!

It's no wonder her reply was full of sarcasm and the irony of the moment: "How is it that You, being a Jew, ask me, a Samaritan [and a] woman, for a drink? For the Jews have nothing to do with the Samaritans" (John 4:9, AMP).

Jesus did not answer with scorn or contempt. He was not insensitive, nor was He rude. Rather, He saw a heart that was thirsting for a different kind of water. He saw that she was open, curious, and longing for fulfillment. His response to her broke down the walls. No one knows better than our creator that we all have a need to feel valued. This woman's need was no less so than ours, and Jesus knew it. He would use her physical thirst to drive home a spiritual principle.

When we partner with God, doing what He is doing and fulfilling His purposes, our lives will have the greatest possible significance, and we will be free to operate in our motivational and other spiritual gifts.

Jesus offered the woman spiritual water, but she misunderstood and thought He meant literal water. Noting He had no equipment with which to draw water from the well, she boldly challenged His claim of having the power to give her this water He had spoken of. Seeing beyond her words into her questioning eyes, Jesus replied that Jacob's well would satisfy only temporarily, but He could give water that would satisfy permanently. His answer could only mean that He considered Himself greater than her religious or cultural traditions. Jesus knew how to get right to the heart of the situation and into the heart of the person.

The Gift of a New Life

Weary of going to the well daily and being parched spiritually, this woman was interested in a permanent solution to her problems. It seems she had been seeking love in all the wrong places. She had at least sought satisfaction through more than one man. Like most women, she was relationship-oriented; she had a deep longing to be loved and accepted. For her, this need had led her down a path of sin.

Before the Samaritan woman could respond fully to the offer Jesus made to her, it was first necessary to deal with her sin. The Scriptures do not say if she was widowed or divorced, but we do know that she had been married five times and was now living with a man who was not her husband. If she was a multidivorced woman, she undoubtedly had experienced a great deal of suffering. Because the Samaritan faith was based on the Pentateuch the woman's husbands would have rejected and divorced her, not vice versa. Can you imagine the pain she must have endured from being rejected by as many as five husbands?

Jesus tactfully brought her to accountability. When He confronted her sin gently by telling her to go get her husband and come back, she answered Him honestly, "I have no husband" (John 4:17). Imagine how she must have felt. Yet she didn't try to cover up her condition or downplay it. And Jesus, in turn, commended her for her truthfulness.

It was then that the unfathomable happened. Jesus revealed to her that He was the Messiah. Right there in Samaria—entirely out of His orthodox cultural setting and with a woman, He proclaimed He was the promised Messiah. Up to this point we have no evidence from

Scripture that Jesus had yet revealed His identity even to His disciples. Clearly Jesus saw worth in this woman and thought her capable of understanding deep spiritual truths. Even though this woman was living in sin, He trusted her with profound truth. He knew she was one who would joyfully operate in her giftedness, thereby reaching many others with the Good News of salvation through Him.

Her heart must have been filled with hope as she dared to believe His words. The promised Messiah stood before her. Her face-to-face encounter with Him had changed her life. Her search for truth had been realized. Now from her innermost being flowed rivers of living water. Now she derived new life from Him. She had just experienced wonder and fascination. She would now be free from shame or fear. And she would feel valued.

Immediately—leaving her water pot behind—the Samaritan woman returned to her city to tell everyone what had happened to her at the well. She had met the Messiah and received the gift of eternal life! Others must meet Him too! Nothing was more important to her than telling others how she had met the Messiah. Scripture tells us that as a result of this woman's testimony, many from her village ran to the well. Because of her proclamation, they too met the Messiah and invited Him to come to their region to teach and disciple them.

WITH THE GIFT COMES A PRICE

We all are called to be partners in the harvest. Just as God used women in Scripture as partners in the harvest, He is calling women today. But there are costs to any call or gift.

When the woman at the well heard the Good News, she immediately left her water pot—a possession precious to her according to the custom of the time. Her abandoned water pot is a prophetic picture of what many of us have to leave behind when we make our commitment of faith and follow the leading of the Lord.

In some Middle Eastern cities, water pots are valuable, not as much monetarily as sentimentally. Because water is equated with life, to leave one's clay water pot behind is like leaving one's soul. In these same cities, where water is often scarce, carriers go through the streets selling water by the drink. And their cry is this: "The gift of God. Who will buy? Who will buy?" Sometimes a wealthy man will offer to buy the whole supply and then allow the water carrier to give it away. At that point the vendor no longer says, "The gift of God. Who will buy?" but "The gift of God. Who will take?"[1]

Team ministry is the New Testament model for fulfilling the Great Commission.

The woman of Samaria received the gift of eternal life and the motivational gift of encouragement. At that point nothing, not even her precious water pot, was more important to her than having met the Messiah and having the opportunity to share her Good News with others.

WHAT ARE ENCOURAGERS LIKE?

Encouragers love to share with others and encourage people to be all they can be. They enjoy giving counsel to others, and they are strongly interested in seeing others grow spiritually. One gift survey shows that 16 percent of Christians have the gift of encouragement.[2] Many translations of the Bible use the terms "exhorter" and "gift of exhortation" to describe this motivational gift and its manifestation. The word *exhort* often connotes urging and warning as well as sharing. Encouragers (or exhorters) tend to be quite verbal. In fact, they are typically better communicators than most people with other motivational gifts. For all of these reasons, they are considered the "mouth" of the body of Christ in the world.

The woman at the well, though she may have been a social embarrassment because of her lifestyle, must have been known in her community as one who spoke her mind. She was apparently well-known enough, credible enough in what she shared, and verbal enough that when she chose to speak, people listened. Scripture records that when she told of meeting this man Jesus the people of her village listened and responded. Her words must have been compelling because many went to see for themselves.

This gifted woman exhibited a few very specific characteristics of an encourager. When she experienced something that changed her life, she was immediately motivated to encourage others to live victoriously. Also typical of encouragers, she was one who found truth in her life through an experience rather than through the Scriptures. The encounter shows she was fairly excitable. After hearing the Good News, she wanted quickly to settle her own spiritual problem and then those of others. Finally, she had a flair for stretching the truth to make her point. Remember when she told the people of her country, "Come, see a man who told me everything I ever did" (John 4:29)?

Another characteristic of encouragers is that they are typically everyday people with life-giving words to share with others. Rick Joyner in his book *Shadows of Things to Come* said, "The real, substantial work of the kingdom is accomplished by the day-by-day faithfulness of average pastors and laypeople…average Christians who are doing great things for the kingdom." He also says that to help the advancement of the kingdom, we do not have to do anything extraordinary. We just have to be obedient and faithful.[3]

The Samaritan woman was certainly just an everyday person trying to make the best of her circumstances. However, after she had been transformed from a social outcast to a gifted follower of Christ, she was fully able to operate in her motivational gift. Because of her past and her face-to-face encounter with Jesus, she would go on to do much more than those of us without her motivational gift or life experiences. Her gift of encouragement, combined with her unusual past, would enable her to offer her life as an undeniable example of God's ability to transform lives.

MODERN-DAY ENCOURAGERS

When my friend and ministry team member Janet encountered Jesus, she—like the woman at the well—immediately wanted her whole world to know of her newfound faith in Christ. She went around telling everyone who would listen that the Bible was true. "I didn't know enough to defend my new convictions at the time, but I wanted to spread the word about this amazing love and dynamic transformation

I had experienced," she told me. "I had to tell everyone: 'It's real. He's alive.' I was powerfully changed.

"My continual encouragement to people was that God would do for every person what He had done for me, if they looked to Him," Janet recalled. "Unlike the woman at the well, I was in the most fulfilling, lovely time of my life. I had a loving husband, I was living in my first home, and I had a healthy infant. What more could anyone want? Yet I felt like everything changed dramatically after I gave my life to Christ, and I wanted the whole world to feel what I was feeling."

Janet has become a leader in our Women With A Mission ministry. Here's how she describes her role. "When I take an inexperienced team overseas to do evangelistic work, I feel like I'm planning a secret birthday party," she explains. "I have this unquenchable grin inside. Every time I watch others realize their God-given giftedness and uniqueness, it's as if we're all celebrating their birthday. When I see people 'open' and use the gifts God has given them, a celebration happens inside me, too. One of my greatest thrills is to encourage others to see Jesus in such a dynamic way that they, like me, can run around telling others, 'It's true, it's true, Jesus is alive!'"

Another modern-day woman with the gift of encouragement and a wonderful sense of humor to boot is Lyn, another ministry team member and an excellent example of someone who loves to encourage those around her and who recognizes and understands the motivational gifts of others. Here's her story.

"Every one of my mission trips has provided wonderful memories, but my first overseas mission trip will always be special to me. With well-planned schedules in hand, we thirteen women took off for the Philippines. That probably doesn't seem like a large team when you realize we were doing two major conferences. However, that many women using two bathrooms for two weeks can stretch even the most merciful personality! Add to that [the fact that] three of the women were perceivers.

"Encouragers can be confronters and fixers, so when tension between a few of the team members became evident, my mind began to click and sort out choices and object lessons to be learned. On this occasion God had other plans. At one point I was caught in the bathroom of one of the bedrooms when the tension came to a head. I decided to stay quiet and out of sight. Just call me a chicken when it isn't my war. Anyway, I listened as words were spoken and forgiveness came. I was stuck in that bathroom for hours as the two settled their differences and chatted! Finally I came out, much to their surprise and my relief.

"If hearing someone talk a lot makes you nervous, don't take an encourager with you when you want to minister to someone. We are called 'the mouth' in the body of Christ. In fact, there have been times when those with the teaching and perceiving gifts have actually told us to shut up. Of course, we don't take offense, because encouragers are not easily offended.

"On another trip I took a group of six women to do three conferences in the Philippines. Early one morning, we met at the airport in Manila to board our plane for Molave, Mindanao, but we found our flight had been cancelled. After much talk, we finally convinced the airport manager that we needed to get to Mindanao that day. We were flown to Dipolog City. From there, we had been assured we could pick up a bus to take us to Ozomos, where our Philippine pastors were waiting to take us to the conference in Molave.

"Arriving in Dipolog City, we found that the bus had already left the airport. Now we were six hours away from our conference and had no way of notifying the pastors in Ozomos. Did that keep this encourager down? Not at all! I just *talked* with the airport manager until he ended up getting us a van and a driver. So off we went in a van driven by a man we didn't know into an area we'd never been, which we learned later was known for its many kidnappings. But nothing could quench our zeal. God in His grace had sent us a Christian driver who got us to the conference one minute before it started. The conference was wonderful and all went according to the plans and purposes of God. Thank you, Lord, for giving me the gift of gab!"

CHALLENGES FOR ENCOURAGERS

The woman of Samaria took no thought for the cost of accepting the truth about Jesus. No doubt some of the villagers misunderstood her proclamation. After all, what would this woman know about truth? Didn't she know that the Jewish Messiah would not have anything to do with a woman like her? The Messiah would come to the religious leaders of the day, wouldn't He?

Some who heard her may have reflected that her verbal boldness was just another attempt for acceptance, another try for yet another man to give her attention. They may have thought she was merely drawing attention to herself.

No doubt some scoffed at her attempt to share about Jesus; with others, criticism and ridicule surely ran high. These responses, however, did not deter her from her mission and from freely operating in her newfound gift.

So it will be for many of us. When we freely operate in our motivational gifts, we may receive ridicule and rejection, not only from unbelievers but also from well-meaning Christians. Their possible misunderstanding of our gifts must not deter us from using them. We must not allow the perceptions and judgments of others to deter us from the call God has placed on our lives and from accomplishing the purposes He has for each of us.

Ministries as well as the refinement of our gifts are birthed from our times of coming face-to-face with Jesus. This spiritual closeness will also produce spiritual fruit. Look at what happened to the Samaritan woman. She spent time with the Messiah, and immediately she began operating in her gift, which, in turn, made way for her community to be evangelized.

Author Frederick Buechner in *Wishful Thinking* said that the place God calls you to is "the place where your deep gladness meets the world's deep need."[4] God does not gift you with talents or gifts merely so you can lavish them on yourself. Your gifts are to be used to serve the body of Christ—and the world.

C. Peter Wagner, in his book *Your Spiritual Gifts Can Help Your Church Grow*, wrote that the gift of encourage-ment (he calls it exhortation) is a person-centered gift. "The gift of exhortation is the special ability that God gives to certain members of the body of Christ to min-ister words of comfort, consolation, encouragement, and counsel to other members of the body in such a way that they feel helped and healed."[5]

Encouragement is a tremendous gift to have. But because it is so people-centered it is easy for the encourager to become overly involved in the lives of many people, and we all know how time-consuming that can be. The encourager, then, needs to be deliberate about spending time with the Lord and developing true fellowship with Him as a priority above all other relationships.

> *God asks us to get out of our comfort zones. Change is essential to growth and development—ours and others'.*

Spending time with your friends or spouse cannot counterfeit your time with the Lord. The woman of Samaria could not receive her true purpose from her husbands. Only when you are alone in God's presence can He reveal Himself and His purposes for you. In these times, your spirit becomes one with the Lord. It is then that you hear His voice, know His ways, and feel His desires and His heartbeat.

The goal of every Christian is to become Christ-centered rather than self-centered. In the case of the encourager, it is to become Christ-centered rather than people-centered. Time with Him does this. He is a faithful, loving God who deals benevolently with you. Daily communion with Him brings correction, counsel, comfort, and confidence. Oneness with the Lord comes only through your prayer times with Him. It is then that the Holy Spirit gently corrects you, guides you, and builds your confidence to accomplish His plan for your life.

When you are able to discern your gifts and your calling and walk in them, you'll be able to have a life filled with peace, joy, and closeness with the Lord. Oswald Chambers wrote: "There is only one relationship that matters and that is your personal relationship to a personal redeemer and Lord. Let everything else go, but maintain that at all costs, and God will fulfill His purpose through your life."[6]

LEAVING MY OWN WATER POT

While living in Portland, Oregon, several years ago, I was involved in numerous women's ministries. My life was crammed with friendships, activities, and purpose. When my husband considered a career change that required a move to Colorado, I was reluctant to relocate. After all, I was comfortable where I was. I was being used by God and was operating quite nicely in the gifts He had imparted to me.

I think we would all agree that change can be difficult, especially as we get older and set in our ways. But God asks us to get out of our comfort zones. Change is essential to growth and development—ours and others'.

As I sought the Lord, He reminded me that Abraham, Moses, Rahab, Ruth, and Naomi all had to leave a country to receive the blessing God had for them. So I agreed to the move. To say that our move to Colorado Springs has greatly enriched my husband's life and mine is an understatement.

How many times have you cried out for the Lord to use you in a greater way only to find yourself facing a change? David said, "You have freed me when I was hemmed in and enlarged me when I was in distress" (Ps. 4:1, AMP). Enlargement comes through pressure!

You too may have to step out—perhaps not physically, but at least emotionally and spiritually. You may have to leave some water pots behind.

Have you left behind some things to follow the Lord and His call on your life? Are there additional "water pots" you may need to give up? People? Belongings? Reputation? Desires? Finances? Time? Ambitions? Career? And the dreaded question for many people who are already in an established work for the Lord: Are you willing to give Him your ministry, too?

THE LEGACY OF THE SAMARITAN WOMAN

It's significant that Scripture doesn't even record the Samaritan woman's name. Unlike other women mentioned in the Bible, her name apparently was not deemed important enough to be recorded. It was her encounter with Jesus and her gift of telling others about Him that mattered most.

Could it be that the woman at the well was the first evangelist for Christ? When we partner with God, doing what He is doing and fulfilling His purposes, our lives will have the greatest possible significance, and we will be free to operate in our motivational and other spiritual gifts.

For Further Thought

1. Do you believe God has given you the gift of encouragement? Explain why or why not.

_____

_____

_____

_____

_____

2. When was the last time you used or saw someone else use the gift of encouragement? Describe how you felt as a result.

_____

_____

_____

_____

3. Describe a time when you witnessed the gift of encouragement being misunderstood.

_____

_____

_____

_____

4. List steps you may need to take to spend more time with the Lord.

_____

_____

_____

_____

CHAPTER 5

BIND US TOGETHER, LORD, BIND US TOGETHER:
Euodia and Syntyche

I wonder, would Euodia and Syntyche (*SIN-ti-kay*), two New Testament women who worked closely with the apostle Paul, have fit quite comfortably on that van ride through Madurai, India, described in Chapter 1? Both women had motivational gifts that they used when they worked together. Why did the apostle Paul call these women out by name in his letter to the Philippians, pleading with them "to agree with each other in the Lord" (Phil. 4:2) and imploring his Christian brothers to "help these women who have contended at my side in the cause of the gospel" (Phil. 4:3)?

A NEW TESTAMENT TEAM

Euodia and Syntyche were powerful women of God and fellow workers with Paul, who described them as team members who had *contended* at his side in the cause of the gospel. The Greek word for contend, *sunethlesan*, is a strong word. It portrays a grueling, competitive athletic combat, like that of gladiators in competition. According to Paul's description, these two women were front and center, alongside one of the greatest ministers the world has ever known. They were partners with him, fighting aggressively to spread the gospel.[1]

In spite of their good work, however, these two women had a relational problem. Evidently it was not simply a private matter, but one that affected the whole Philippian church. It appears they did not esteem each other, at least at the time of Paul's writing. Perhaps each was comparing herself with the other. Whatever the issue, it was serious enough that Paul addressed it in a public letter, asking the rest of his fellow workers to help the two women resolve their differences.

CHALLENGES OF TEAM MINISTRY

Team ministry is the New Testament model for fulfilling the Great Commission. Jesus and His disciples worked together as a team during the three years of His ministry. The apostle Paul tells us that Jesus Himself put together a team for developing unity and maturity of the saints. "It is he who gave some to be apostles, some to be prophets, some to be evangelists, and some to be pastors and teachers, to prepare God's people for works of service, so that the body of Christ may be built up until we all reach unity in the faith and in the knowledge of the Son of God and become mature, attaining to the whole measure of the fullness of Christ" (Eph. 4:11–13).

Paul's own ministry team was as diverse as the team of disciples Jesus brought together. In fact, Paul's team encompassed people from two continents. It crossed racial, social, cultural, and gender barriers. At a minimum, Paul's team included a theologian, an aristocrat, a prophet, a pastor, a businesswoman, tentmakers, a doctor, and a teacher.

If you take a closer look at these New Testament teams, you will discover each one had its problems. Even among members of the "dream team" Jesus put together there was disagreement. Remember when His disciples argued about who would be the greatest in the kingdom? (See Mark 9:33–37.) And who can dispute that there were differences among Paul's team members?

In addition to the problems between Euodia and Syntyche, there is at least one well-documented account of a heated argument between Paul and Barnabas. (See Acts 15:37–40.) Paul and Barnabas had been partners in ministry for years. We know that Paul was a teacher and Barnabas, whose name actually means "encourager," was just that. Barnabas actually mentored Paul and introduced him to the disciples. Together, these two were powerful, successful missionaries. However, after starting their second missionary trip together, they got into a major disagreement over young John Mark, cousin of Barnabas. In this case, their division over the issue actually led to separation! The result was that Paul took Silas with him, and Barnabas took John Mark.

Although we have little insight into what was going on between Euodia and Syntyche's team members, we can speculate. My first supposition is that their motivational gifts were totally different, and I believe each had strong convictions of how to work in ministry. In team ministry, the possibilities for conflict are great, partly because of the differences in our gifts and how we evaluate and approach various situations. It was true in the apostle Paul's time; it appears to be true with the team of Euodia and Syntyche; and it's true in my own Women With A Mission teams. Even the best of teams are going to experience conflict.

WHAT ARE PERCEIVERS LIKE?

Up to this point in our study, we have looked at women whose motivational gifts were obvious, evident to all as they went about their daily lives and worked with others in ministry. Though we have only hints of what Euodia's and Syntyche's gifts were, their story points us toward an examination of two particular gifts, perceiving and administration. I will explain later in this chapter why I believe Euodia and Syntyche possessed these two gifts. Perceiving—the gift above all others that seems to act as a catalyst for conflict in teams—may have been Euodia's gift. In the next chapter we will examine the gift of administration, which may have been Syntyche's gift.

Although the gift of perceiving and the word *prophecy* are often used synonymously, this is a good time to differentiate between the two for the purpose of our study. Because the same Greek word, *propheteia*, is used in all three lists of gifts mentioned in chapter 1, the gift of perceiving can easily be confused with either the manifestation gift of prophecy or the ministry gift of prophet to the church. Don and Katie Fortune stated, "In the specific context of motivational gifts we see that the Word refers to one who is especially sensitive to perceiving the will of God and then proclaiming it—or, depending upon the

Lord's direction, praying for it to be accomplished. The perceiver then is one who readily perceives, prays about, proclaims, and promotes the will of God."[2] Perceivers are aptly labeled the "eyes" of the body of Christ.

Because perceivers believe the will of God has been revealed to them, they are very confident in their perceptions and decisive about what should be done. Perceivers have a special ability to proclaim God's truth without compromise, and they are quick to discern spiritual issues. Perceivers also tend to be strong-willed. These qualities can be a setup for conflict among team members if perceivers' insights and contributions are not appropriately valued and addressed.

Because our gift study so far has given us clearer pictures of three of the seven motivational gifts—serving, mercy giving, and encouraging—it might be helpful to see other very specific characteristics of perceivers by contrasting them with other gifts.

A perceiver:

❖ "Just knows" when something is true, whereas a mercy giver knows truth through her spirit's response to what she hears and sees.

❖ Tends to see issues as black-and-white, whereas an *encourager* has a tendency to see most sides of issues.

❖ Tends to be a loner, whereas *encouragers* and *mercy givers* need other people for affirmation.

❖ Is motivated to make decisions based on what's right, but an *administrator* (see chapter 6) will make a decision based on what will accomplish the agreed-upon goal.

As we examine the motivational gifts of administrator, teacher, and contributor in the remaining chapters of this book, the following gift characteristics will become clearer to you:

❖ A *perceiver* is generally much less conservative about life than a *teacher*.

❖ An *administrator* wants order and organization, but a *mercy giver* wants to keep everybody happy.

❖ A *teacher* bases theology on the written Word of God, while an *encourager* places high value on personal religious experience.

❖ A *contributor* might make a decision based on what is good financially, whereas a *teacher* might want a decision to be based on what is theologically sound.

❖ A *server* is very pragmatic about her faith, which is the opposite of a *teacher*, who considers ideas and doctrine more important.

❖ An *encourager* likes new things and can easily accommodate changes, whereas a *teacher* tends to want things to stay the way they are.

Can you see the tensions that can develop among people with different motivational gifts? Add to the potential for conflict our different temperaments, cultural backgrounds, personal preferences, and education, and—

no doubt—many conflicts can arise in team ministry.

We can see that perceivers, administrators, and teachers display the strongest convictions. People with these gifts tend to be "black vs. white" and believe that it would be compromise to acquiesce. People with the other four gifts—those who are servers, mercy givers, encouragers, and contributors—tend to be more flexible. Because Euodia and Syntyche were experiencing difficulty in resolving their issues, it is reasonable to assume their gifts were perceiving, administration, or teaching. Otherwise, one woman would have yielded to the convictions of the other before it became necessary for Paul to take their issue before the entire church.

Let's take this analysis further. An encourager would not have deemed the problem worth fighting over because it could not affect things eternally. A server simply would have removed herself from the situation in favor of more practical actions. A contributor would have been seriously concerned only if the problem had to do with finances. And a mercy giver, always considerate of the feelings of others, would not have wanted conflict of any kind. We can go a step further and eliminate teacher as a gift either of these women possessed because Paul—a teacher himself—does not point out doctrinal differences as the issue between Euodia and Syntyche. That assumption leaves us with two choices—perceiver and administrator. I suspect that one of the women was a perceiver and one was an administrator.

A perceiver tends to be spiritually discerning, strong-willed, and very direct in speaking. An administrator wants to be the boss, is very organized, and usually has a plan. You can easily see how this mix of gifts in ministry could bring conflict or, at the least, a difference in how things are perceived.

I do not want to leave the discussion about perceivers without acknowledging that perceivers often do express prophetic words and have dreams for themselves or others. I have benefited from this aspect of perceivers many times.

In 1996, at the very beginning stages of Women With A Mission's outreach to India, a friend and I spent a few days together enjoying a lovely golf course with mountains off to one side in Welches, Oregon. One morning we were praying for India, which was the nation of the day as part of the Praying Through the 10/40 Window program.

The sky was clear, but as we prayed a cloud came down upon the main mountain peak just outside our bay window, covered it like a hat, and then moved down the mountain and took the shape of a tube surrounding it. The cloud then began to move around the mountain in a way that was similar to a hula-hoop motion. It was an interesting sight.

At the time, the political situation in India was unstable. And, to our knowledge there were no teams of women going to that nation. My friend became excited about this sign and believed that the Lord would "take the nation," just as the tube was going around this mountain.

I felt that the Lord had shown me that I would be taking teams around India, just as the tube was going around the mountain. There was a quickening in my spirit, however, I thought, "I am willing to go, Lord. However, I don't know anyone who ministers there." We concluded our time.

In April 1998, a friend who is not only a strong perceiver but also one of the few prophets I know personally, called to relate a dream she had just experienced. Through the years she has not only had dreams for me but also interpreted many of my dreams. In her dream I was going into a new geographical area, and I met a man who was smaller and darker than I. She awoke then. As she related the dream to me, she began to prophesy that not only would I meet this man soon but that I was to quickly follow his leading even though I did not know anything about him. Further, she said that God was in it and that as I walked with Him the Lord would rise to meet me and I would do miraculous things, as well as open new doors. She went on to say that outreach would be a pioneering effort for Women With A Mission.

The next October I was invited to the home of friends Mary and Terry, where I met a man whose description fit the man in her dream. He was the president of India Gospel League, a powerful multi-ministry organization. Immediately we both knew God had brought us together to partner on behalf of the women of India.

The next October, in 1999, Women With A Mission made its first trip to India. To date, our teams have trained more than ten thousand women in India to minister in their own nation with a goal set for fifty thousand women to be reached by 2005. This friend's words to me were prophetic indeed.

A MODERN-DAY
EUODIA-AND-SYNTYCHE TEAM

Other than the fact that Wilma and Betty, a missionary team in the Philippines, are both unmarried women and both share a love for music, they are extremely different, primarily because of their contrasting motivational gifts. Wilma is a strong perceiver (which is tempered by her gift of serving), and by the time she was five years old she was already aware of God's work in her life. Betty, on the other hand, is a strong administrator (influenced by her second gift of exhortation) who made her commitment to Christ as a teenager.

Wilma and Betty, at times, could very well fit the apostle Paul's description of Euodia and Syntyche. Wilma is one who discerns things rather quickly and then is ready to jump in and get the job done. To those who don't know her well, it can appear that she is impulsive, pushy, and somewhat unpredictable. In contrast, Betty (the administrator) is very orderly and analytical. She makes lists and is slow to act. After a decision is made, however, she is enthusiastic about it and is a great encourager (exhorter). She is verbal, and she is rather predictable.

Despite their differing gifts, Wilma and Betty have partnered with each other successfully for more than twenty years to promote the kingdom of God in the Philippines. They are powerful, nation-changing women. But because of their differing gifts, this partnership has not been without its difficulties.

For example, Wilma just wants to get the job done any way she can. She is quick to make decisions. As a perceiver, she has strong ideas and tends to be uncompromising. Conversely, Betty is always planning and organizing. She is methodical, and, because she is an administrator, she believes she knows the best way to reach a goal. Can you see how their relationship could be fractured from time to time?

So, how have Wilma and Betty been so successful for all these years? They say that success comes by making it a priority to develop trust, honor, and respect for each other.

"What is your secret for unity?" I asked them.

Betty's reply was: "If we are to be effective servants on the mission field, we must learn how the Lord would deal with this problem. The answer is respect! There must be respect for the other person's ministry gift if you expect to operate effectively as a team."

Wilma and Betty have come to recognize and respect the truth that we all "know in part" (1 Cor. 13:12). In addition, they have equal concern for each other. They acknowledge that each has received different spiritual gifts and that they, as women in partnership for the Lord, complement each other by employing their gifts in love. Wilma and Betty have made a covenant with each other to lay aside their own agendas for the greater cause. They have learned the art of developing character. Because they have set aside their individual differences, they have become successful together in their work for the Lord.

A MODERN-DAY PERCEIVER

Jan does a wonderful job as a Bible-study leader. She has a profound way of discerning and then explaining spiritual truths. On one occasion she had two encouragers in her Bible-study group who constantly interrupted her teaching. Encouragers are like that. They love to talk!

Week after week this went on. One day, in sheer frustration, Jan spoke out, half jokingly, "Would you ladies please shut up!"

That was one of my first experiences of observing a frustrated perceiver! Jan had spiritual points to make and spiritual principles to impart; therefore, she had less tolerance for distractions than others in her role might have had. If the women there with me at that moment had not understood the motivational gifts and known Jan's heart, then the incident might have been an opportunity for offense and division.

A noted Bible teacher once said that rebuke without relationship brings rebellion. Thank goodness all of us in that Bible-study group were in relationship. As those women yielded to Jan, the entire group grew spiritually.

As you interact with others in the body of Christ, be sure of this: there will be possibility for conflict along the way. If you see the conflict as negative and insulting, you may inhibit your own influence in the work God has called you to do. But if you see the conflict as an opportunity to grow and to appreciate the differences in the people God places you with, then the very conflict can bring growth and maturity into your life. Working together with others who are gifted differently from you can bring fullness and balance to the body of Christ.

BUILDING MULTIGIFTED TEAMS

Because each woman on a team brings a special and unique strength for accomplishing a task, motivational gifts are a huge consideration when I select members for my Women With A Mission teams. We all are needed to accomplish the work of the ministry. I look for women who, working together, embody the seven gifts so the team will function fully and have the same balance as the body of Christ.

I learned this team-building principle from my husband's experience in business. As CEO of several semiconductor-chip companies, he has needed to hire many management teams. He always fills those positions with men who know more about their particular area of responsibility than he does. Why? Because it is key to the success of the business! Their styles, knowledge, and strengths vary, and the results are strong management teams—and strong companies.

> *Those with different motivational gifts know things I need to know. In contrast, I know things they need to know. Each of us has unique revelations that enhance the others' knowledge of God.*

I love the brainstorming and strength women draw from one another's gifts when they are brought together in multigifted teams. Together we are able to apply the whole counsel of God. Those with different motivational gifts know things I need to know. In contrast, I know things they need to know. Each of us has unique revelations that enhance the others' knowledge of God. We all have weaknesses where others have strengths. So as we work properly in our motivational gifts, we complement one another. Together we are a powerful team.

THE LEGACY OF EUODIA AND SYNTYCHE

Even with their relational dilemma, Euodia and Syntyche leave a positive legacy for us today. Yes, they had their problems, but together they still played a major role alongside the apostle Paul in gathering the harvest. Thankfully, we do not have to wait until we're perfect to affect our world!

"Though it costs all you have, get understanding" (Prov. 4:7). We must understand how the body of Christ works to be effectual in our day. We need one another. We need to make ourselves dependent on one another, dependent on our differing gifts. We need the strength of a unified body. This is a clarion call for today.

For Further Thought

1. Directly or by process of elimination, are you able to discern your own motivational gift or those of other Christians you know? What do you base your conclusions on?

_____

_____

_____

_____

2. Do you believe you are a perceiver? Why? To support your answer, give examples of how you operate in the body of Christ.

_____

_____

_____

_____

3. Describe a time when someone with the motivational gift of perceiving used her gift in an extraordinary way to bring unity in the body of Christ.

_____

_____

_____

_____

4. Recall a time when your motivational gift, whatever it happens to be, rubbed against another Christian's gift and caused strife in the body of Christ. How was it resolved?

_____

_____

_____

_____

CHAPTER 6

JUMP INTO THE RIVER:
Lydia

The river—a symbol of life and a place where blessings flow—is where we first meet Lydia, a God-fearing Gentile businesswoman and a seeker of truth. She was just one among the many women who had gathered at the river that day, but she was the woman whose response to the message of salvation would open the city of Philippi to the life-giving waters of the gospel of Christ.

At the river, vegetation is often lush and life-giving. We can imagine those who had come there jumping into the river and soaking in its coolness. In Bible times the river was considered a holy place, a sacred place, a place of rejoicing. Some scholars say it was customary for places of prayer to be located outdoors near running water.[1] Surely the river was a place where these women felt God's presence in the beauty of His creation. Is it any wonder, then, that Lydia and her friends had gathered there to seek God?

A SABBATH ENCOUNTER

In Acts 16:13–15 we read Luke's words about Lydia's meeting with Paul and those who accompanied him. "On the Sabbath we went outside the city gate to the river, where we expected to find a place of prayer. We sat down and began to speak to the women who had gathered there. One of those listening was a woman named Lydia, a dealer in purple cloth from the city of Thyatira, who was a worshiper of God. The Lord opened her heart to respond to Paul's message. When she and the members of her household were baptized, she invited us to her home. 'If you consider me a believer in the Lord,' she said, 'come and stay at my house.' And she persuaded us."

We know that Lydia made an immediate, crucial, and intentional decision.

Although Lydia was a native of Thyatira (Turkey) at the time of this Sabbath encounter, she was residing in Philippi, a Roman colony in Macedonia (a country north of Greece). Philippi was a city of sophistication and culture, a prosperous city with a great deal of political clout, pride, and privilege.[2] Philippi also was famous for a purple dye that came from the murex, a shellfish found in the Ganges (Gangites) River that flowed about a mile from the city.[3] Lydia, a commercial dealer in purple cloth and apparently a prominent woman of the city—she was the only woman at the river who was named by Luke—made her living from a by-product of the dye.

The apostle Paul's primary evangelistic strategy for reaching Jewish people with the gospel was to teach at the local synagogues on the Sabbath. By the time he reached Philippi, his approach already had proved effective in reaching many faithful Jewish men and women with the message of the new covenant of Christ Jesus. In Philippi, however, despite the size of the Jewish population and sophistication of the city (or perhaps because of it), the Jews did not have the requisite quorum of ten reliable men to form a synagogue.[4] Because there was no synagogue, Paul and his entourage proceeded to where the devout ones of the Jewish faith were said to gather—at the river.

Can you imagine the scene? Lydia and her friends are sitting by the river studying the Scriptures and learning from the Talmud. Enter Paul and his companions Timothy, Silas, and Luke. They greet the women and address them in the manner consistent with their culture. Paul's convincing words that day about Jesus being the Messiah must have been like a cool drink from that river, bringing refreshment and life to their thirsty souls.

Perhaps the men spoke of how the river was like God's mercy and love flowing to them through His Son Jesus. Or perhaps they spoke of how God's salvation and healing were like a river of life flowing from the heavenly sanctuary. They may have used the river to symbolize the life-giving blood of Jesus, which cleanses all from sin.

Whatever approach Paul used, his words brought new and powerful concepts to Lydia and those who were with her that day. We know that Lydia made an immediate, crucial, and intentional decision. She, along with her household, were baptized right there in the same river. She then persuaded Paul's entourage to stay at her home. We can guess that she was hungry to know more about the Lord and grateful for these guests to her city who had led her to the truth.

FIRST EUROPEAN CONVERT

Lydia's name in the Greek means "bending," and she certainly lived up to it that day by bending before the Lord and His apostles to receive salvation. The significance of her riverside encounter with Paul was huge to the spread of the Christian faith. Lydia became the first convert in Europe, and she played an important role in pioneering the establishment of the church in Greece.[5]

We can assume that Lydia's cloth-making and marketing business was challenging and time-consuming, yet we see immediately she was a determined woman who wanted to grow spiritually. That is evident from her insistent appeal to Paul and his friends to stay at her home. She obviously was a forceful woman who didn't take no for an answer and was comfortable being in the forefront. Because her response to God's call on her life was immediate and was followed by decisive, long-term, life-changing action, God exalted her and used her motivational gift of administration to help build His kingdom.

Whether Lydia was widowed or single, we do not know. We do know that no life partner is mentioned in Scripture. Being a romantic at heart, I love C. Peter Wagner's take on the "unwritten" ending of the story about Lydia. Wagner makes this contention because Luke's narrative in Acts changes from "we" to "they." (See Acts 16:40.) When Silas, Paul, and Timothy departed Philippi, Luke must have stayed behind. As further proof, Wagner suggests that the "loyal yokefellow" referred to in Philippians 4:3 is in fact Luke the physician. Several commentators, F. F. Bruce among them, agree.[6]

Did Luke stay in Philippi and marry Lydia, becoming her partner in all matters related to the development of the church in that region? In his commentary on the Book of Acts, Wagner wrote: "Of course, the romantic notion I earlier proposed, that Luke and Lydia might have married, cannot be definitively proved or disproved by the text itself. It is up to our individual imaginations."[7]

Regardless, we do know the church flourished, as is evident from Paul's letter to the Philippian church twelve years later thanking them for their missionary support. (See Philippians 4:15–16.) In this letter it is apparent that this church was a great source of consolation to Paul while he was in prison.

WHAT ARE ADMINISTRATORS LIKE?

Administrators are referred to as the "shoulders" of the body of Christ. What do the shoulders of our bodies do? They hold up our heads and give our bodies the stability we need to function. Those who have this gift shoulder the church with their skills of organization, management, and responsibility.

Lydia's gift as an administrator presents itself in the details of this story. Administrators are able to make quick decisions. Immediately upon her acceptance of the Good News, Lydia added decisive action to her faith. She invited Paul and his friends to her home to stay. The events recorded in subsequent verses of Acts 16 indicate the duration of the stay was considerable.

Scripture says Lydia persuaded the apostle Paul. Can you imagine the scene? We can surmise that after hearing the truth, Lydia wanted more teaching and acted decisively to reach her goal. We know she was a prominent woman of the city. Her persuasive appeal must have felt to Paul like an open door for the ministry he hoped could be birthed in that city.

Administrators are goal-oriented strategizers. We can certainly see Lydia's strategies falling into place in this story. First she accepted Paul's message and was converted. Apparently following her lead, the rest of her household made commitments of faith as well. They were already at the river, so why not proceed to be baptized as well? Next, most logically, would be for these messengers of the gospel to return to Lydia's home so she could have them share her new faith with the rest of her family and household.

> *Whatever your hand finds to do,*
> *do it with all your might.*
> — *Ecclesiastes 9:10*

Administrators are good managers of time, money, people, and resources. We already know Lydia was a prominent businesswoman, a dealer in purple cloth. She must have had a large home, ample enough to accommodate all these men. Her "household" mentioned in Acts 16 most likely consisted of personal attendants and servants as well as family. Later we see in Paul's writings that a house church was established. Her household was Philippi's first congregation and she its first convert and leader under the training and leadership of the apostle Paul himself.

Lydia, like Deborah, was willing to move into something totally new and lead others there as well.

Administrators exercise effective management skills. During the early years of Israel's existence as a nation (see the Book of Judges), there were cyclical times of blessing, peace, and favor; backsliding and sin; oppression from nefarious enemies; humility, repentance, and redemption; and deliverance and blessing. The particular cycle the nation was in directly correlated to the god it served. During the times of backsliding and sin, everyone "did that which was right in his own eyes" (Judg. 21:25, KJV). Recalcitrant, these people eventually abandoned the very God who had blessed them.

As a result Israel's enemies oppressed them. It is during one of these periods of time that we meet another great administrator—Deborah. A few of her roles were wife of Lappidoth, judge, stateswoman, prophetess (see Judges 4), composer of a masterpiece of Hebrew poetry and song (see Judges 5), singer, mediator, and counselor. One wonders how she did it all.

During Deborah's rule as judge, the Canaanites oppressed the Israelites. Through her administrative gift, she was able to conceive a strategic plan for defeating the enemy. She was able to see the larger picture. Realizing the dire straits her nation was in, she decided to step into the unknown. Although she had never been to war, she was willing to lead the army into battle for her nation. So great was her stature among the people that Barak, head of the troops, refused to go to battle without her personally at his side. (See Judges 4.) Her strategic planning and leadership, directed of course by the Holy Spirit, resulted in a great victory for Israel.

Lydia, like Deborah, was willing to move into something totally new and lead others there as well. As a result, she was significant in establishing the kingdom of God in Greece, previously a spiritually dark region.

A MODERN-DAY ADMINISTRATOR

Pat is a woman filled with endless energy. On any given day, you will find her busy managing her husband's office operations, home-schooling her daughter Amanda, planning fund-raising events for her church, writing articles for publication, and being the consummate homemaker. She and her husband, Gregg, are also small-group leaders at their church.

Pat wears many hats. How does she do it all? Simply put, she has the gift of administration.

Like others with this gift, Pat always has several balls in the air. She's a strategizer, and she enjoys being at the epicenter of activities. Pat is goal-oriented and delights in accomplishing tasks efficiently. She is never seen without her daily list of things to do. I have observed her manage several projects simultaneously with great joy and ease. Pat loves accomplishing tasks so that the kingdom of God prospers. If you ask her, she will say that it is her mandate in life.

As a team member on one of Women With A Mission's trips to Africa, Pat exercised her gift of administration in ways that made her invaluable. On that particular mission, our team consisted of fifteen women, which was a large group to manage. We anticipated that the trip would be particularly complex because we planned to travel to several countries in Africa. Knowing Pat's gift of administration, I asked her to help me manage the team by jumping in whenever she saw a need. She accepted with great zeal and enthusiasm!

You can imagine the logistics of managing paperwork and passports when going through customs; overseeing the tickets, seat assignments, and boarding passes; making sure all airport fees were paid; arranging for laundry to be done; and ensuring that effective communication about trip details occurred between me and the other team members. And those were just a few of Pat's responsibilities! To my great delight, she kept me and the entire team on track and on time wherever we went.

Daily we had several ministry projects to accomplish, some occurring simultaneously, and they all required organization. Pat kept track of all of the women, monitoring their schedules and making sure their efforts all fit into the bigger picture. To my amazement, she collected praise reports along the way and somehow found time to communicate them regularly to our intercessory team and husbands back home. Upon our return to the United States,

I used her detailed journal of our experiences to prepare a newsletter describing the events and successes of our trip.

CHALLENGES FOR ADMINISTRATORS

As incredible as this motivational gift is to the church, it can bring with it a unique set of challenges. Often people with this gift are overly concerned about the tasks at hand and can overlook the human element, which in turn causes others to misinterpret their actions. Pat's use of her gift on our team trip to Africa serves as an example. While some members of our team recognized and appreciated Pat's organizational skills, others misinterpreted them as her "taking over" or being "pushy" even though she was doing only what I had agreed with her was needed.

Administrators often can seem to be more task oriented than people oriented. In carrying out her responsibilities, Pat came across to some team members as being insensitive to their feelings. Because she was concerned about getting the tasks done, intent on staying focused and stressed by the pressures of the moment, she was, at times, more direct in her approach than she might have been in other, less demanding situations.

This is yet another example of how important it is to balance our motivational gifts with the fruit of the Spirit, mainly love and self-control. At the same time, however, it is the responsibility of maturing Christians to learn to recognize the characteristics of each motivational gift as it is displayed and to allow grace to all those who are walking in their gifts.

In the previous chapter, we noted that perceivers, administrators, and teachers display the strongest convictions. This chapter helps us see how critical to the bigger picture is the role of those who exercise administrative skills. In the next chapter, we will factor the skills of teachers into the fully functioning body of Christ and ministry teams.

THE LEGACY OF LYDIA

Lydia is a role model for women today. She was undoubtedly a woman of strength, boldness, and determination. Certainly she experienced stress and time management concerns just as today's women in leadership do. Having boldly accepted Christ, she quite probably found unique opportunities to witness about her faith to her buyers, an action that could have put her and her business at risk. Although we know of many who were persecuted for their faith (Paul names several in his letters), we see no indication that Paul was concerned about either Lydia's ability to resist the pressure or the fear she must have faced.

Lydia appears not to be fearful about the cost of her faith or about using her gift. Like Lydia and Deborah, we need to be willing to move into new territories for God, no matter what spiritual gifts we possess but especially if our gift is administration. God is looking for women who will follow Him. He needs women who will "jump into the river."

Perhaps you recognize yourself in this chapter, either as one who possesses the motivational gift of administration or as one who has misunderstood the use of the gift.

Do you find yourself taking the lead in groups? Do you have the ability to see long-range objectives and carry them through? Are you one who makes lists to oversee effectively all the matters involved in a project? Do you find yourself unhappy or complaining when things are not organized? Then your motivational gift for ministry may be administration.

If so, consider yourself in good company. Eve; Joseph, the son of Jacob; Nehemiah; David; James, the brother of Jesus; and of course Lydia and Deborah were all administrators.

For Further Thought

1. Describe how you know if you do or don't have the motivational gift of administration.

   _____

   _____

   _____

   _____

   _____

2. Describe a time when you have seen the gift of administration used effectively.

   _____

   _____

   _____

   _____

3. Describe a time when you may have seen the gift of administration misunderstood.

   _____

   _____

   _____

   _____

4. If you have the gift of administration, describe how you are able to use it in your home, church, or community.

_____

_____

_____

_____

_____

CHAPTER 7

TEACH US YOUR WAYS, O LORD:
Priscilla

Businesswoman, church planter, teacher of leaders, and teacher to the nations. Does this description sound like a twenty-first-century woman? In fact, her name was Priscilla, and she lived in the first century A.D.

Priscilla was a well-known, gifted, and influential woman. References to her appear in four different books of the New Testament. Each time we hear about her she was working hard—working alongside her husband, Aquila, in their tentmaking business; working alongside the apostle Paul in evangelism and discipleship ministry; personally instructing Apollos, a prominent orator, to equip him for ministry; and leading churches that met in her home.

Her life offers us both an inspiring picture of a godly woman and also an opportunity to take a closer look at the motivational gift of teaching.

A WOMAN OF THE WORLD

We first meet Priscilla in Acts 18. At the time she and her husband were living in Corinth (Greece). Aquila was originally from Pontus in northern Asia Minor and thought to have been a freed slave. He lived in Rome long enough to win his freedom and a wife.[1] He relocated to Rome and met Priscilla. They soon had a thriving business as tentmakers. As a result of the edict of Claudius Caesar that banished the Jewish colony from Rome in approximately 49–50 A.D., they again relocated to Greece. (See Acts 18:1–2.) Scripture indicates that Priscilla was in the business of tentmaking along with her husband.

It is here in Corinth that Priscilla and Aquila met the apostle Paul during his second missionary journey. In the absence of any mention of Priscilla and Aquila being converted under Paul's ministry, we can assume they were already believers. Some scholars believe Priscilla and Aquila were charter members of the church in Rome, so their relocation to Corinth would have provided excellent support for new church planting in Greece. Whatever the circumstances of their meeting with Paul, it seems this prosperous Jewish couple was impressed enough by the apostle to invite him into their home.

Both Paul's and Aquila's profession, passed on to them by their fathers, was making tents and leather goods. Tentmaking was a lucrative trade, since tents were at the very core of the culture. Tents were used for open markets, conducting various businesses at the city gates, and of course traveling. Tentmakers were important contractors in their day.

Paul, finding himself alone in Corinth after recently parting from Silas and Timothy, most likely was in need of money. (See Acts 17:14.) Upon meeting Priscilla and

Aquila, he offers his skills to Aquila. Not only was tent-making an expedient way for the apostle to support himself in ministry, but it appears his partnership with Priscilla and Aquila was mutually beneficial. We see that they, too, use their trade as a means for ministry.

A WOMAN OF MINISTRY

Priscilla, Aquila, and Paul must have been in tune spiritu-ally as well as professionally. Scripture says that Paul lived with Priscilla and Aquila for eighteen months, resulting in the establishment of a great work in the Corinth church. We learn in Paul's first letter to the Corinthians that a large, vigorous church was established as a result of their alliance. Their ongoing importance to Paul personally and in ministry is revealed other places in Scripture. In three different epistles, Paul puts them at the top of his list of people who are to receive his greetings. (See Romans 16:3; 1 Corinthians 16:19; 2 Timothy 4:19.)

Priscilla's ministry must have given her wide acclaim. Five out of the seven times that Priscilla is spoken about in Scripture, her name is mentioned first before Aquila's. This is noteworthy, since the sequential order was impor-tant in biblical narratives. Customarily, the man's name was written first. The fact that Priscilla's name appears before that of her husband is a clear statement of Priscilla's importance. Perhaps she was more outgoing than Aquila, or maybe she was the prominent ministry leader in their home. It is safe to assume that, since her name is typi-cally given first, Priscilla was recognized by the readers of Paul's writings as the more influential of the two.

John Chrysostom, a great preacher and church father from Antioch in the fourth century wrote this of Priscilla:

> This, too, is worthy of inquiry, why, as he addressed them, Paul has placed Priscilla before her husband. For he did not say, "Greet Aquila and Priscilla," but "Priscilla and Aquila." He does not do this without reason, but he seems to me to acknowledge a greater godliness for her than for her husband. What I said is not guesswork, because it is possible to learn this from the Book of Acts. [Priscilla] took Apollos, an eloquent man and powerful in the Scriptures, but knowing only the baptism of John; and she instructed in the way of the Lord and made him a teacher brought to completion (Acts 18:24–26).[2]

Whatever the reason Priscilla is mentioned before her husband, we can read between the lines and understand that her prominence also speaks of her character. It is obvious that Aquila approved and promoted God's calling on her life. Scripture is clear that both of them worked together in the business of tentmaking and in ministry. There is no hint of strife between them. Together, they affected their generation for Christ.

Priscilla surely must have enjoyed the knowledge gained from the nightly dialogues with Aquila and Paul in her home. A teacher herself, she would have enjoyed the authority and range of experience of the apostle's teaching. Can you imagine the privilege of sitting at the feet of the apostle Paul, gaining spiritual wisdom, for eighteen months? What a divine opportunity! After Paul had gone from Corinth, the importance of those eighteen months to the ongoing church in Corinth bears fruit in the ministry of Priscilla and Aquila. In Romans 16, Paul refers to Priscilla and Aquila as "fellow workers in Christ Jesus."

When it was time for Paul to sail for Syria, we learn that their personal and ministry bond was such that the couple accompanied Paul on his journey as far as Ephesus. (See Acts 18:18.) Paul stayed in this area a short time before continuing on to Jerusalem, while Priscilla and Aquila remained in Ephesus. We can assume that here, too, like in Rome and Corinth, they put their gifts to work in the planting and growing of churches.

Ephesus was not an easy place to win people to Christ. It was the third largest city in the Roman Empire and known for its decadence, idolatry, and financial prowess. The Temple of Diana (Artemis), known as one of the Seven Wonders of the World, had great influence spiritually, financially, and sensually. Ephesus was situated in the middle of the trade route between the eastern and western Mediterranean, making it strategic for business. Notice the impact of their ministry here. Priscilla and Aquila played a key part in winning the people of this city to Christ. According to Acts 19:10, in a matter of only two years the entire region of Asia had heard the word of the Lord.

We know that Priscilla and Aquila were partners in Paul's apostolic team. In addition to her individual endeavors, it is evident that Priscilla was an effective team member. Over and over we see Paul praising her for her sacrifice. Never do we see evidence of reluctance on her part. We see her accompanying her husband in three countries and several cities, which made them an international team of ministers. They were a unique cross-cultural team.

I believe that Aquila was a supportive and encouraging husband to Priscilla, helping her develop her own gifts as much as she was a helper and partner to him. Women in ministry know the importance of having husbands who support them, whether that work is in the nursery, teaching a Sunday school class, preaching, or doing missionary outreach around the world.

Priscilla must have possessed an amazing flexibility. She would have had to put up with disruptions in her home as she hosted Paul and others who met there for teaching, putting the needs of others before her own. In addition to sharing what she owned, she would have had to bear the cost of these efforts in time, energy, and money. As a woman in business and ministry, she would have had to deal with the pressures and perplexities of the diversity of her activities.

How many times have you moved in your life? How many times to other countries? Relocating to different cities and countries would have necessitated Priscilla's adjusting to different cultures and people as well. As we follow her in Scripture, we see that she actually moved her home four times and helped establish churches each time.

WHAT ARE TEACHERS LIKE?

Those with the gift of teaching delight in reading and studying. It is the foundation of their efforts. Teachers of the Word of God recognize the Scriptures as the highest authority. The teaching of the Word with accuracy and in a systematic way is very important to them, not only in their own teaching opportunities but also in the teachings of others.

After traveling from Corinth with Paul and establishing residence in Ephesus, Priscilla and Aquila attended synagogue one Sabbath. Speaking this day was a young, brilliant Jewish man from Alexandria (Egypt). He spoke with great zeal and fervor. He was well learned, cultured, and eloquent. He also knew Scripture thoroughly. (See Acts 18:24–25.) How impressive Apollos must have been. How taken the audience would have been with his dissertation. It is said of him that by using Scripture, he greatly refuted the Jews, arguing that Jesus was the Christ.

Priscilla the teacher, however, had strong convictions and opinions based upon her own investigation of Scripture and the facts. She noticed that his knowledge of the work of Christ was incomplete. Teachers are like that. They really want preaching and teaching to be delivered with accuracy and in context! And, remember, at this point she had already spent time under the tutelage of the apostle Paul.

Early church leaders rebaptized those who had been baptized before the cross.[3] Apollos was teaching regarding the water baptism of John the Baptist. But Apollos was ignorant regarding the baptism of Christ's death, burial, and resurrection. (See Acts 18:25.) Apollos was teaching repentance by water baptism, and Priscilla wanted to correct him regarding the baptism into the name of the Lord Jesus—being baptized into the community of believers by Jesus' name. (See Acts 19:5.)

Priscilla was bold but self-controlled (another trait of teachers) as she invited Apollos into her home. Luke clearly states that she, along with Aquila, proceeded to instruct him in the greater truth of the gospel. (See Acts 18:26.) This gift into his life was significant. She helped launch his apostolic ministry. In essence, she multiplied herself by empowering Apollos for a more effective ministry. As a result of her mentorship, Apollos enjoyed a faith-building experience. He was surely indebted to her theological instruction and mentorship, and the whole of Asia Minor benefited by it.

Have you noticed this characteristic of those you know with the gift of teaching? Because they are scholars of the Word, they find themselves wanting to correct the facts presented by others and point out other improvements.

Noted author and teacher Marilyn Hickey, whose life demonstrates that she most definitely has the gift of teaching, tells the story of the time she was listening to a speaker who was talking on and on.[4] Marilyn felt like she was getting nothing out of his talk. The notebook she used for taking notes was empty. Distressed, she looked around and noticed that others in attendance were spellbound by the speaker. Marilyn questioned the Lord, who told her that she should be hearing with her spirit and not her head! She said she learned a lesson that day, that she can receive something from any speaker no matter the speaker's style or method of teaching.

Marilyn's initial reaction was natural for a person with the motivational gift of teaching. Teachers are definitely more objective than subjective. Learning is important to them. They want their notebooks full of notes!

Education, too, is important to teachers. Look at the teachers you know in the church. Aren't they the ones who are always going to seminars and conferences, taking courses to expand their Bible knowledge? Unlike encouragers, who may have only a few themes and not many teaching points while speaking, teachers are prolific in putting forth observations.

The motivational gift of teaching enables teachers to take difficult concepts and make them simple and understandable. For example, on our recent missions trip to Fiji, Marnie tackled the complicated theme of reconciliation and taught with principles anyone could comprehend. She began her message with Isaiah 58:12: "Your people will rebuild the ancient ruins and will raise up the age-old foundations; you will be called Repairer of Broken Walls, Restorer of Streets with Dwellings."

I watched as she taught point-by-point on the aspects of how we rebuild, repair, and restore relationships. I was amazed not only at her teaching style but also at the profound words she was speaking. I found myself wanting to stop and meditate on all of her points. Because of Marnie's simple approach and the organized way in which she presented what could be an elusive topic, I still recall the principles she presented to this day.

SUSANNA WESLEY AND THE GIFT OF TEACHING

When I think about great women with the gift of teaching, I think of Susanna Wesley. She bore nineteen children, including John and Charles, and is considered the mother of Methodism. Mrs. Wesley preached to more than two hundred people every week in prayer meetings, which she led in her husband's parish. No wonder her son John used woman leaders for the small groups called "classes," which spread their revival so effectively.[5]

Mrs. Wesley had great courage in difficult times. She was reportedly pretty and bright, yet poor and frail. Being a woman of strong discipline, she made it her daily routine to spend two hours in prayer and six hours educating her nineteen children every day. She was the ultimate homeschooling parent! In her "household school," it is said of her that she taught her children so thoroughly that they became unusually cultured. There was not one of them in whom she did not instill a passion for learning and righteousness.[6]

Even with the constraints of teaching on her time, Mrs. Wesley found the time she needed to pray. An amusing story is told of her pulling her apron up over her head, which became her prayer closet. When she did this, her children knew not to disturb their praying mother. It's also noted that even when she was elderly, her son John still came to her for counsel.[7]

A MODERN-DAY TEACHER

Sandy is a partner of mine in ministry with a strong teaching gift. She relates a story of how her motivational gift of teaching caused her to react in an incident with one of her daughters.

Sandy shares that a candle on the dinner table had been burning for a long time, and a wide pool of liquid paraffin floated atop the eight-inch pillar. Leslie, age eight, was bored with adult dinner conversation and dipped her spoon into the puddle's depth; three-quarters of an inch of clear, glowing wax dripped from her silverware. Tiny fingers collected the spoon's bounty and rolled the wax into a pebble, adding to the line of pebbles on the table.

"Leslie, stop playing with that wax. It's hot! Why don't you just blow out that flame?" Sandy asked.

Leslie stood up, bent over the candle, and poof! She blew straight down, and then it happened. Out went the flame and up flew the paraffin. Yes, up! And it coated Leslie's eyelashes, her nose, and her lips. "Ouch, ouch, ouch!" the little girl squealed.

"Oh, honey!" Dad's voice pained with her plight. Turning to Sandy, he pleaded, "Go minister to her."

Sandy arose and quickly began peeling away bits of wax, and then she began to "minister."

If you have the gift of teaching and love to research, learn facts, and instruct others, it is important to develop a godly awareness of the people with whom you are working.

"The next time you blow out a candle, hold it directly in front of you, like this," she said. "Then, as you blow it out, be sure you are safely puffing horizontally so that the wax will go away from your face and not into it."

Dad strained anxiously forward in his chair. "No, no, no! Just HUG her!" he pleaded. His mercy heart ached.

Meanwhile, older daughter Sarah, whose gift is serving, quickly stood up. "Oh, can I get you a cool washcloth for your face, Leslie? Do I need to get any wax off the carpet?" she offered.

Each member of Sandy's family moves in a different God-given motivational gift. Dad's heart is very comforting to others. His is the gift of mercy. Sandy teaches to the point that at times her children will stop her and ask her to just listen and not give wisdom or instruction. Sarah is ever alert to any need that she might serve. Other gifts in their family include perceiver and giver.

To some without the teaching gift, Sandy's reaction to her little girl's dilemma might appear as though she were lecturing or being insensitive. In reality, she was using her teaching gift to instruct her child for future protection.

CHALLENGES FOR TEACHERS

Do you or women you know listen to audiotapes, read books, or want to correct the one giving the Sunday morning sermon? Do you enjoy sharing your knowledge and expertise? Do you seek out persons who you know you could help in the development of their gifts or ministry? These are evidence of the motivational gift of teaching. This is a gift with the potential of great impact on others to the furthering of their ministries. It is also a gift that must be tempered with love.

If you have the gift of teaching and love to research, learn facts, and instruct others, it is important to develop a godly awareness of the people with whom you are working. They are probably not teachers. Because of your desire to train with completeness, you may be tempted to tell everything you know. At times it is possible that they may think of you as boring. If you do not take the time to inspire them, they may lose interest.

Teaching is one of my gifts. It is always a temptation to present voluminous material when I am speaking in a gathering or even relating an incident. My husband often asks, "What is your point?" My response is, "This is the point. It just takes me a while to get to it!"

Here's another caution for teachers: because you love to study and gain knowledge, you may be tempted to become prideful. Scripture says, "Knowledge puffs up, but love builds up" (1 Cor. 8:1). In other words, loving those around you is more important than instructing them if it comes to a choice between the two.

PRISCILLA'S LEGACY

Our final glimpse of Priscilla in the Scriptures is in 2 Timothy 4:19 where the apostle Paul sends his greetings to Priscilla and Aquila who are in Ephesus working with Timothy. This epistle was penned years after Priscilla and Aquila worked side by side with Paul, yet he still is greeting his dear friends of many years. His commendation of honor and the fact that Priscilla's name is the first one on the list of people to whom Paul sends greetings reinforce his admiration for Priscilla publicly. This passage alone should be enough for us to want to take careful notice of her qualities as displayed in Scripture and imagine the aspects of her character that made her so effective.

I imagine Priscilla was a woman sensitive to God's voice, desiring to be ever faithful regarding the gifts and callings God had given her. I can also imagine that she was humble, always encouraging others. She must have been a devoted wife and friend, one sought out for her wisdom, passionate about work and ministry, determined to persevere in every circumstance. She was hospitable, and she was a servant. Most importantly of all, I see her as one who ministered in strength.

I believe that Priscilla was a woman who understood and respected headship. Her relationship with her husband as copartners in business and ministry must have been an incredible example to others. And, her adaptability to the changes in hers and Aquila's lives illustrates that she was able to be content wherever she was. Often, I am asked if I like living where I do. My answer is always, "As long as I am with my husband, and we are in a good church, I'm happy!" I believe Priscilla felt that way too.

I also believe that Priscilla recognized the proper way to work within the role of the women in her day. She must have recognized order, authority, and loyalty, and her devotion to both Aquila and ministry is evident. If she did not possess these godly qualities, she could not figure so prominently in Scripture.

Priscilla was not unlike the Proverbs 31 woman. She was a woman of noble character. She was invaluable to her husband and held in high esteem by others. She was a businesswoman. She could serve and entertain people in her home. She had a good reputation and was wise, not lazy. She had power and authority. She met the needs of her family. While Scripture does not speak of her having children, had she bore any, they surely would have called her blessed.

Is teaching a gift you have but have not yet developed? Look at your talents in light of the attributes of the gift. What are you passionate about? Where do you see a need and feel an urge to help meet it?

You may be thinking, "I'm not Priscilla, with the gift of teaching and all of her other attributes." You may feel like you lack the ability you see in her to accomplish a task. Or maybe you just don't know yet what it is that God is asking you to do for the kingdom of God. Not all of us have the same calling as Priscilla on our lives. Her unique challenges and obstacles are not ours either. We all, however, have a call on our lives from the Lord.

The Scripture comes to mind, "Whatever your hand finds to do, do it with all your might" (Eccles. 9:10). Another verse is the prophet Elijah's asking the widow woman, "What do you have in your house?" followed by an admonition to use it. (See 2 Kings 4:1–7.) God does not require anything of us that we are not able to do by His power. He has given each of us something we can take and use to meet a need. What do you have "in your house" that can be given to God for multiplication?

For Further Thought

1. Do you have the desire to make sure things are completed in a well-structured, logical way? Explain. How do you think you could use these qualities to minister to others?

_____

_____

_____

_____

2. Recall a time when you knew information being taught was inaccurate. How did you react?

_____

_____

_____

3. Whether or not you have the motivational gift of teaching, would you be willing to homeschool your children or grandchildren should it become necessary? Explain.

_____

_____

_____

_____

_____

4. Describe a time when the motivational gift of teaching caused you or someone else with the gift of teaching to be misunderstood. How was the matter resolved?

_____

_____

_____

_____

_____

Chapter 8

THANK YOU FOR GIVING TO THE LORD:
Phoebe

As a child, did you ever put together jigsaw puzzles? Do you remember searching through all the hundreds of pieces and finding just the right piece to go into a certain spot as you watched the picture unfold? Oh, yes! Well, that's somewhat how we are going to put this picture together of Phoebe, a biblical woman who had the motivational gift of contributing.

Phoebe is mentioned only once in Scripture. Here's what the apostle Paul says about her in Romans 16:1–2: "I commend to you our sister Phoebe, a servant of the church in Cenchrea. I ask you to receive her in the Lord in a way worthy of the saints and to give her any help she may need from you, for she has been a great help to many people, including me." A mere fifty-three words declare her contribution to the spreading of the gospel and the building of the kingdom.

As I researched the details of Paul's writings, I garnered much more information about Phoebe. I also found pieces to our puzzle by studying history and the records of the church fathers. In so doing, I found Phoebe to be a rare kind of woman worthy of our attention.

PHOEBE TRAVELS TO THE CHURCHES IN ROME

Phoebe, a pagan name meaning "bright" or "radiant," is the feminine version of the name Apollo. Her given name, therefore, indicates that she was a Gentile and not a Jew by birth. We do not know where or when she was converted. By Paul's strong recommendation of her, however, we can safely say she was one of his trustworthy coworkers.

Phoebe most likely was once a worshiper of the pagan Grecian gods. When Paul mentions her, she was a worshiper of the Living God and Paul's true "sister." Her conversion and willingness to use her motivational gift took her to a higher level of living—one of being a "sent one" by the apostle Paul and one who experienced the word of the Lord spoken in Jeremiah 29:11: "'For I know the plans I have for you,' declares the LORD, 'plans to prosper you and not to harm you, plans to give you hope and a future.'"

What specifically did Phoebe do in ministry with Paul for the Roman churches? Paul had anticipated a visit to Rome many times, but he was forced to delay his long desired visit for many years. (See Acts 19:21.) As a result, it appears he dared to make his initial contact with Roman believers through Phoebe. From the fifty-three words written of her, we can deduce that she was the one who carried Paul's letter to many of the Christian congregations in Rome. Paul's choice of Phoebe for this work shows his tremendous trust in her.

Why would Paul ask Phoebe to carry this very important letter to Rome? Several reasons come to mind. She was from Cenchrea, a seaport about seven miles east of Corinth, which was an eastern port. Paul wrote the letter to the Romans from Gaius's home in Corinth. John Polhill, in his article "Paul and the Romans," states that Paul "probably wrote Romans from Corinth during his last three-month stay in Greece."[1] (See Acts 20:1–3.) Here is where Paul likely met Phoebe and where he learned of Phoebe's position, not only in the church but in her community as well.

Some scholars think Phoebe was a single businesswoman and that foreign travel was not unusual for her. Perhaps she traveled to Rome often to conduct business and thereby knew many in the area. This might have been another reason why Paul entrusted Phoebe with his letter.

Phoebe's task of delivering Paul's letter from Corinth to Rome meant she would have to carry the message over land and sea, which was no easy task. Just the thought of the physical demands of traveling in those days is staggering. Even today, with all of our modern travel conveniences, it's a tiring experience.

Travel by sea was fraught with danger, as we can see in the many Bible stories of sea travel. Besides the many dangers such as thieves or muggers that awaited any traveler over the mountains, Christianity was unpopular in Rome. Christians were not welcomed there. I'm sure Phoebe knew that her choice would come with a cost. The fact that she successfully carried out this task shows incredible boldness, strength, and courage on her part.

In Romans 16, Paul greets twenty-eight leaders in the house churches by name, ten of whom are women. Notice that he commends Phoebe to them as one who deserves to be esteemed and helped in any way possible. She obviously had a heart to serve and certainly a heart to give.

In verse 1 Paul calls her a servant. According to Jouette M. Bassler in the book *Women in Scripture,* "The Greek word for minister (or servant) here is *diakonos,* or deacon. It implies that Phoebe had the same status in the early church as Stephen the martyr and Philip the evangelist. In speaking of Phoebe, Paul also uses the Greek word *prostates,* which some scholars say means leader, overseer, or someone with stature, responsibility and authority."[2]

Bassler says that Phoebe is described also with the word *prostatis,* which is the feminine form of a noun that can denote a position as leader, president, presiding officer, guardian, or patron. Because Phoebe is presented as *prostatis* "to many people, including me" (Rom. 16:2) and not specifically as *prostatis* of the church, the emphasis is probably on her role as patron or benefactor, though the title also reinforces the concept of authority conveyed by the position of deacon.

Paul must have taken notice of Phoebe as a careful and capable manager.

As a patron, Phoebe would have provided funds for her church and probably publicly represented it when necessary. She also would have used her influence—derived from wealth and social standing—to resolve any difficulties that might have arisen for the congregation. Paul said that he himself was personally indebted to her in some way, and he asked the Roman church to help him repay that debt by providing her with a generous welcome and whatever support she required. Paul must have taken notice of Phoebe as a careful and capable manager. And, to Paul's credit, he was willing to release her into a new ministry.

Knowing all these pieces of the puzzle, it's not surprising that the apostle entrusted the care of this precious letter, which is the most elaborate theological essay in the entire book of the Bible, to Phoebe. We know now the weight of his decision. Romans is the most complete declaration of the gospel. From Rome the letter spread to the world, and it's from this letter that we Christians have derived most of our basic doctrine.

WHAT ARE CONTRIBUTORS LIKE?

According to Don and Katie Fortune's research data on distribution of motivational gifts in the body of Christ, only 6 percent of people have the gift of contributing. Compare that figure to mercy givers, which is 30 percent.[3] From my own experience in ministry, I agree that the motivational gift of contributing is rare. However, it is an extremely important gift as it relates to spreading the message of the kingdom of God. This gift is likened to the "arms" of the body of Christ because it carries the load of the kingdom.

Contributors give as the Holy Spirit leads. They give freely of themselves and their resources. Obviously they are good stewards of their resources. They are frugal and use wisdom in all of their financial dealings, which enables them in part to be generous givers. Contributors often look for confirmation on the amount to give and to whom to give.

"For she has been a great help to many people, including me," Paul said. Apparently Phoebe was a giver not only of time and energy to aid Paul in ministry but also of money. Otherwise, she would have been unable to help in a way so significant that Paul thinks it worthy of mention here.

A MODERN-DAY CONTRIBUTOR

I met Melonie in Southern California at an Aglow meeting many years ago. The first thing I noticed about her was her red hair, her height, and her stature. She was and is a real eye-catcher. During the meeting she saw that someone at the table where we were sitting needed a pen. She gave the woman her own pen, taking no thought of whether or not there was another one for herself somewhere. While it might not seem like a big thing to give someone your pen, the way Melonie gave it—with no hesitation—immediately gave me insight into her giving heart.

I have for years observed Melonie as a contributor: financially supporting Bible college students in both the Philippines and Swaziland, supporting pastors in Bible colleges, paying rent for pastors when needed, raising and giving funds for a Christian library in Fiji, financing people to go to the mission field on short-term mission trips, paying tuition for pastors' children, buying large numbers of Bibles for those who could not afford them, "sowing" cars into other peoples' ministries, giving away furniture to those less fortunate, sharing her clothes with others on the mission field, and permitting many people to live in her home for long periods of time.

These are just a few ways Melonie has used her gift of contributing to bless others and extend the work of the kingdom. On one occasion she and her husband actually refinanced their home so she could participate in a missions trip and give so that others could go too.

Those who have the gift of contributing should take note of something important Melonie practiced in the exercise of her gift. While her gift is always evident and often spontaneous, her husband is well aware of it and is a partner with her in her decisions. Likewise, she is always considerate of his agreement with her choices about giving.

Cheri, another Women With A Mission team member, was once the recipient of Melonie's giving. Here is her story:

> I can remember Melonie's generosity toward me on two separate occasions. One was in relation to a missions trip we shared together in the Philippines. We had been back in the United States for approximately two months when Lana asked the team to gather at her home for dinner, a time of evaluation and to share pictures and memories of our trip.
>
> It was just marvelous seeing everyone again, exchanging hugs and stories, feeling so very fortunate for the opportunity and privilege to partner together in the field. As Melonie and I sat on the sofa together, sorting through stacks of pictures and remembering precious people and precious moments, I could not help but notice the beautiful watch she was wearing. I complimented her on it, and instantly, without hesitation, she pulled the watch off and gave it to me. Her action caught me completely off

guard. I remember stammering something like: "I can't take that. I just thought it was pretty!" She, however, insisted I keep it. In amazement, I did.

CHALLENGES FOR CONTRIBUTORS

Certainly the gift of contributing is an essential part of the church at large. Without finances little would be accomplished. Contributors obviously recognize this. If they aren't careful, however, this can become a source of pride for them. In desiring to see that their money is used wisely, they can develop a tendency to want to control the funds they give. In addition, contributors need to make an extra effort to keep their thoughts pure when they see others— who may or may not have the gift of contributing—give finances or other resources.

As I mentioned previously, Phoebe's trip to Rome was dangerous, yet there is no indication in Scripture that she hesitated. She must have been willing, if needed, to give her life. Her journey reminds me of a dangerous and blessed experience of one of our Women With A Mission teams.

A few years ago, members of our team were in the tea country (on the mountaintops) of Sri Lanka. Our daily drive through winding hills and steep roads to our conference site took a little over an hour. The morning drives were beautiful, but the nightly drives back were often cold, rainy, or foggy.

One particular night we were unusually late returning to our base. The fog was extremely dense. It felt eerie. I noticed our van driver was uneasy and quite nervous. His hands were restless on the steering wheel, and he was constantly looking around. Most of our team members were sleeping. Two of us were awake, and we too felt uneasy. When I noticed that the other woman, who had the gift of perceiving, was praying, I quickly joined in. Something was wrong, and we sensed it.

After the conference was over and we were well down the mountain on our way back to the capital city, Colombo, I asked our driver why he was obviously uneasy on our drive back to our base that night. He informed me that Sri Lanka had been in civil war for many years, and that night we were in a dangerous rebel area. We were in the local Tamil revolutionary area, where rebels reportedly stopped cars and vans at night, stealing anything of value to finance their cause. Often they kidnapped someone who could bring a ransom. The driver had been worried for our safety.

A wonderful side note to this story is that I was privileged to introduce our driver to the Lord, who later shared something with me that had been a true witness to him of God's hand on us. He said as a result of the Lord "hiding" and protecting us in the fog that night (and for the rain the other nights, as the rebels would not come out in the rain), he was convinced that we served a greater God than the god of the rebels! He said he learned that Jesus is a strong and powerful God.

Our team's story makes me wonder what stories Phoebe could have told of the Lord's deliverance during her dangerous trek in delivering Paul's letter to the Romans.

PHOEBE'S LEGACY

Phoebe's life is reminiscent of the Scriptures. Matthew 10:8 says, "Freely you have received, freely give." Proverbs 21:26 says, "The righteous give without sparing." Phoebe entrusted herself and her personal assets to others. Undoubtedly she experienced pressure and perplexity, challenge and danger, but her gift of contributing directed her to value the needs of others above her own.

Freely you have received, freely give.
— Matthew 10:8

I once heard someone say that opportunities are "pregnant places of promise." I like that. We too, like Phoebe, can take advantage of opportunities that come our way, opportunities that will result in the fulfillment of our calling and destiny. Like all the biblical and modern-day women described in this book, we can move into those pregnant places of promise where God can use our motivational gifts.

Do you see yourself in any of the examples of contributors in this chapter? Perhaps you are part of the 6 percent who have the rare and unique gift of contributing. Maybe you do not have money to give, but you often give your possessions to others and truly enjoy sharing what you have with them.

Do you believe God is your source and, therefore, do not worry about your lack? Do you find yourself trying to motivate others to give? Do you try to control the money you do give? Perhaps you get upset when others do not give. If you answered yes to more than one of these questions, you may have the motivational gift of contributing. If you do, I wonder what pregnant places of promise await you as you let God use you to further His kingdom.

125

For Further Thought

1. Would you say that you have the gift of contributing? Explain.

_____

_____

_____

_____

_____

2. Name a time when you, like Cheri, received something of value from someone who had the motivational gift of contributing. How did you respond and how did it make you feel?

_____

_____

_____

_____

3. Would you agree or disagree that the gift of contributing is a rare gift? Explain.

_____

_____

_____

_____

4. If you have the gift of contributing, what do you enjoying giving to others (besides money) or doing for them?

_____

_____

_____

_____

_____

_____

CHAPTER 9

IN PERFECT HARMONY

It was spring 2003. Nine Women With A Mission team members were in China. Our plans had been laid out carefully, and the schedule was set. Due to circumstances beyond our control, however, our plans abruptly changed. The SARS epidemic had just hit the news. We were on an unknown path.

Each day as we waited for the Holy Spirit's direction, wonderful and exciting opportunities came our way. These unexpected opportunities ultimately led to many people coming to Christ.

On one occasion we accepted an invitation to visit the home of a young female engineer. Also in the home were the engineer's mother, her small child, and the child's nanny. As conversation flowed, the reason for our coming to China came up. We shared our purpose, and the young woman wanted to hear more. What happened next is a wonderful example of how our motivational gifts were manifested and how they worked together in perfect harmony.

The perceiver on our team, who had noticed a sadness about the woman, said to her, "I would like to share a thought with you that I believe is from God. May I?"

"Certainly," the young woman replied. The thoughts the perceiver shared made it seem as if she were reading the engineer's mind.

The team's encourager stepped in next and started sharing some of her own experiences of childhood. She said that as a young girl she had struggled with self-esteem and unresolved issues that had carried over into her adulthood. Her problems resulted in anorexia and bulimia, which took their toll on her—physically, emotionally, and spiritually.

Next the teacher of the group shared her life story with the young woman. Each of these women in her own way (and through her unique motivational gift) shared how God had redeemed her life.

Touched by all she was hearing, the engineer began to cry. One of the team members then presented the plan of salvation to her, and she invited the Lord into her heart and life.

All of the gifts are vitally important in God's economy of accomplishing His works in this world through His saints.

As this amazing encounter unfolded, our team's mercy giver quietly played a game with the woman's young child on the other side of the room. Our server was silently going around helping with refreshments for everyone. From her chair across the room, our administrator watched and prayed silently, making sure all was done in an orderly fashion.

I am so thankful that each woman that day knew her place in the body and how to minister in her own special way. There was not one hint of competition or disagreement among the women as each one operated in her unique gift. As a result, before the end of the evening the engineer, her mother, and her daughter all came to Christ.

GIFTS OF EQUAL VALUE

As this experience shows, all of the gifts are vitally important in God's economy of accomplishing His works in this world through His saints. While some of the gifts, such as serving, teaching, administration, and perceiving, might be more visible and more easily identified, all of the gifts are equal in value to the Lord. In this story the work of several of the motivational gifts was needed to accomplish God's plan. And all of us shared equally in the blessing of having been used in our gifts.

Here are some *dos* to keep in mind while you are maturing in your gift:

❖ Do become comfortable in the gift God has given you.

❖ Do allow your gift to come forth.

❖ Do look for ways in your home and community, perhaps even on the mission field, to use your gift.

❖ Do temper your gift with God's fruit of the Spirit—love, joy, peace, patience, kindness, goodness, faithfulness, gentleness, and self-control. (See Galatians 5:22–23.)

❖ Do prepare to use your gift by frequently spending time in the Word and in prayer.

❖ Do ask the Lord for opportunities to use your gift.

❖ Do become aware of how you respond to certain situations based on your motivational gift.

❖ Do respect the gifts of others.

Here are some *don'ts* to keep in mind while you are maturing in your gift:

❖ Don't covet someone else's gift.

❖ Don't criticize someone else's gift.

❖ Don't use your gift as an excuse for poor behavior or poor decision making.

❖ Don't use your gift to enable the poor behavior or poor decision making of others.

❖ Don't judge others' gifts based on your gift.

THE DANGER OF JUDGING

The final entry in this list of *don'ts* deserves some explanation. Often, if we aren't careful, our strength can become a weakness when we judge others' actions through the magnifying glass of our own gift. Here are some examples:

❖ *Perceivers* have a difficult time understanding why everyone doesn't see spiritual things the way they do. They sometimes think others are compromising.

- ❖ *Servers,* who love to minister to the physical needs of others, can't see why everyone doesn't automatically respond to these types of needs.

- ❖ *Encouragers* just want everyone to get along, so they tend to be critical of everyone else for not extending enough grace.

- ❖ *Teachers* expect presentations of the Word to be done systematically, so they have difficulty listening when someone with a nonteaching gift is trying to explain or teach them something.

- ❖ *Administrators* can't understand why everyone else can't see all the needs that must be addressed in an orderly way to reach a common goal.

- ❖ *Contributors* tend to evaluate the worth of people by what others give in time, money, and resources. Contributors often are put out if other people don't just naturally give as much as they do.

- ❖ *Mercy givers* can't comprehend why everyone isn't more sensitive to the feelings of others.

Do you see when we judge others by our own unique gifts that division and strife can enter the work God has called us to do in our homes, communities, and around the world? God did not intend for this to happen. He didn't give one gift more value than another; therefore, neither should we.

JESUS, THE FULLNESS OF ALL THE GIFTS

Jesus is the fullness of all the gifts. We have many examples of this in Scripture. Following are just a few examples, but you can find many more in your own study of Scripture. In fact, you may be most in tune to examples that match your own gift.

Jesus is the fullness of all the gifts.

We can see Jesus' *serving* gift perfectly displayed when He took the towel and washed Peter's feet. (See John 13: 4–9.) Of course His coming to the world to "destroy the devil's work" (1 John 3:8) assuredly was the greatest act of service to all humanity for all of time.

In Luke 7:11–15 we read about Jesus passing through Nain. There He spotted a funeral procession near the town gate. He worked His way through the crowd until He came upon a widowed mother whose young son had recently died. Jesus knew that more than just a life had been cut short; He also recognized the provision for this woman's care and future was gone too. His mercy-giving heart went out to her. He said to her, "Don't cry." Then He proceeded to raise her son from the dead.

Jesus comforted His disciples with the gift of *encouraging* when He prepared them for His return to heaven. That day He said to them, "Do not let your hearts be troubled. Trust in God; trust also in me. In my Father's house are many rooms; if it were not so, I would have told you. I am going there to prepare a place for you. And if I go and prepare a place for you, I will come back and

133

take you to be with me that you also may be where I am" (John 14:1–3).

Notice how Jesus' *perceiving* gift manifested itself when the Jewish leaders brought a woman to him who had been caught in the act of adultery. (See John 8:3–11.) Jesus did not approve of the stoning because it was apparent to him that those calling for it had impure motives. He recognized their pharisaic judgment against the woman, and He let them know of His insight in a very peaceful way—by writing on the ground with His finger. As He did so, one by one they began leaving. This gift of perceiving saved a life that day!

While speaking to the heavenly Father in what is commonly known as His high priestly prayer, Jesus says, "I have brought you glory on earth by completing the work you gave me to do" (John 17:4). As the supreme *Administrator*, Jesus had a job to do and put together a team and a plan to accomplish it.

As Jesus instructed the crowd on the mountainside near the Sea of Galilee, He used His *teaching* gift. (See Matthew 5:1–12.) We know this portion of Scripture as the Beatitudes. As a result, today we have a written record of what I once heard called the "constitution of kingdom principles" by which we all can live.

Remember Jesus' offer of living water to the woman at the well? "If you knew the gift of God and who it is that asks you for a drink, you would have asked him and he would have given you living water" (John 4:10). Of course by giving His earthly life upon the cross for you and me, so we could experience eternal life, Jesus exhibited His gift of *contributing*. "For the wages of sin is death, but the gift of

God is eternal life in Christ Jesus our Lord" (Rom. 6:23). What greater gift could anyone ever give?

YOUR MOTIVATIONAL GIFT

God expressed Himself to the world through Jesus. Today He expresses Himself though the gifts He has given you and me. Have you honored His gift to you and used that gift as it was intended—for service and outreach?

Other than the test at the back of this book or any number of tests available to help you discover your motivational gift, here are other ways to determine how God has gifted you:

❖ Start responding to whatever God has put in your life and see where He leads you.

❖ Ask yourself what you are passionate about and then find needs in that area.

❖ Ask others what strengths they see in you. Their answers may serve to direct you to areas of ministry you are well suited for.

What if you believe that your gift is being stifled? Here's some encouragement. Patty had made several attempts to serve in her local church. She had tried working on a number of projects and had attended several events to see if she felt drawn to certain ministries. It seemed that nothing fit her. Not being able to contribute to the church in this way caused her to feel unfulfilled.

Patty took the gift test, which confirmed her motivational gift of teaching. So she began to seek outlets for this gift. She discovered a local Christian program designed to allow women to mentor young mothers. Patty decided she'd give it a try. It turned out to be a match! She now enjoys meeting weekly with a young mother for the purpose of teaching her the Bible and mentoring her in motherhood.

If you, like Patty, know what your motivational gift is but are having trouble putting it to use in your church, consider looking into your community for ways to use it. You may walk through a door God has planned for you from the beginning of time, into ministry far greater than what you would have done had you limited yourself to your home or church!

Remember, your goal is to emulate Christ, who is the fullness of all of the gifts, and to be a faithful manager of what He has given you for service and outreach—in your home, in your community, and in the world.

I, Lana, pray for you and for every woman whose hands touch this book, that by reading it you will find your rightful place in the body of Christ and walk freely in your gifts.

Answer the following questions by placing the appropriate number in the boxes to the right.	Often (3)	Some (2)	Little (1)	Never (0)
1. I am distressed when I see others compromise biblical truth.				
2. I enjoy performing practical tasks that, in turn, help others.				
3. Using my own material for presentations is preferred over that of using another person's.				
4. I love to assist and encourage someone who lacks self-confidence.				
5. I live below my financial means in order to help the church.				
6. Identifying resources and people for the completion of a task is comfortable for me.				
7. I do not want to hurt others' feelings, so I choose my words carefully.				
8. I tend to be strong-willed and see things in black and white.				
9. I prefer being a follower and to let others lead.				
10. I am able to make difficult scriptural passages easy for others to understand.				
11. Information without application makes me unhappy.				
12. Making sure the bills are paid is important to me.				
13. I know God's direction for a group of people.				
14. The comfort of others is very important to me.				

Answer the following questions by placing the appropriate number in the boxes to the right	Often (3)	Some (2)	Little (1)	Never (0)
15. I feel I know what God is saying, and I feel compelled to tell people.				
16. When I see a practical job that needs to be done, I make myself available.				
17. I like to analyze new information.				
18. If a person does not respond to my counsel, I tend to move on.				
19. In order to have money for God's work, I budget carefully.				
20. I enjoy ensuring that rules are followed for maximum efficiency.				
21. People are usually drawn to me because I am sensitive to their hurts.				
22. It is important for me to communicate my feelings.				
23. I have difficulty saying no even when I am already busy.				
24. I am able to take difficult concepts and make them easy for others to understand.				
25. Affirming people is a delight for me.				
26. When I give money, I like to know where it goes.				
27. In order to reach a common goal, people easily follow me.				
28. I enjoy taking a meal to someone who is sick.				

Answer the following questions by placing the appropriate number in the boxes to the right	Often (3)	Some (2)	Little (1)	Never (0)
29. I am able to correctly judge character in others.				
30. I prefer helping people even before being asked.				
31. I love to research answers to prove the truth.				
32. I love giving step-by-step instructions to people seeking advice.				
33. I prefer that my giving be done anonymously.				
34. I want projects to be done correctly, and I know the right people for the job.				
35. I am empathetic to people who are very glad or sad.				
36. In a crowd, I can quickly discern the spiritual atmosphere.				
37. I want my motivational gift to be used in the most effective way.				
38. I am very interested in learning, and I tend to have more study projects than I should.				
39. I am a "people person," and I love feedback when I am talking to them.				
40. Knowing that the Lord is my source, I give sacrificially and freely of my income.				
41. People have told me that I am well-organized.				
42. I am able to internalize my personal hurts.				

Answer the following questions by placing the appropriate number in the boxes to the right	Often (3)	Some (2)	Little (1)	Never (0)
43. I am fearless when speaking the truth.				
44. My ministry is to take the load off leaders by doing any job necessary.				
45. Accuracy in details is important to me.				
46. I believe my counsel to be compassionate and wise.				
47. I take pleasure in being charitable to worthy causes.				
48. I tend to expect everyone on a project to be as committed as I am.				
49. I do not like to confront sin, especially when dealing with those who are hurting.				
50. I can understand the sins and problems of people with whom I interact.				
51. I enjoy being asked to do things at the church.				
52. I tend to read manuals, menus, and books carefully.				
53. I am more interested in information for practical use rather than for ideas.				
54. I feel guilty when I can't give for the building project.				
55. If no leader is apparent, I will volunteer to coordinate a project.				

Answer the following questions by placing the appropriate number in the boxes to the right	Often (3)	Some (2)	Little (1)	Never (0)
56. I am sensitive to people suffering from mental or emotional pain.				
57. I tend to have few close friends as a result of my high standards.				
58. I enjoy short-term rather than long-term tasks.				
59. I use too much information in presenting materials.				
60. People say they have received personal direction after talking with me.				
61. I enjoy helping people (with potential) who are struggling financially.				
62. I employ lists to arrange my schedule.				
63. I am drawn to comfort the poor, downtrodden, and others who have less than I.				

Gift	Total	INSERT POINTS FROM EACH ANSWER								
Prophecy		1	8	15	22	29	36	43	50	57
Serving		2	9	16	23	30	37	44	51	58
Teaching		3	10	17	24	31	38	45	52	59
Exhortation		4	11	18	25	32	39	46	53	60
Contributing		5	12	19	26	33	40	47	54	61
Administration		6	13	20	27	34	41	48	55	62
Mercy		7	14	21	28	35	42	49	56	63

1. In each numbered block place the number you recorded for the question that corresponds to the number in the block.

2. Add all your recorded numbers going across the rows. For example, for the Prophecy row, add the numbers recorded for questions 1, 8, 15, 22, 29, 36, 43, 50, and 57.

3. Write the total for the row in the "Total" column.

4. The three top totals identify your significant gifts.

SUGGESTED READING

Boehme, Ron. *If God Has a Plan for My Life, Why Can't I Find It?* Seattle, WA: YWAM Publishing, 1992.

Brown, Judy L. *Women Ministers According to Scripture.* Kearney, NE: Morris Publishing, 1996.

Cunningham, Loren and David Joel Hamilton with Janice Rogers. *Why Not Women?* Seattle, WA: YWAM Publishing, 2000.

Ford, Paul R. *Discovering Your Ministry Identity.* Mobilizing Spiritual Gifts Series. St. Charles, IL: Church Smart Resources, 1998.

Fortune, Don and Katie. *Discover Your God-Given Gifts.* Grand Rapids, MI: Chosen Books, 1987.

Hickey, Marilyn. *Know Your Ministry.* Denver, CO: Marilyn Hickey Ministries, 1986.

Lutz, Lorry. *Women as Risk-Takers for God.* Grand Rapids, MI: Baker Books, 1997.

Rogers, Adrian. *Unwrapping Your Spiritual Gift.* Memphis, TN: Life Worth Living Ministries, 2001.

Schwarz, Christian A. *The 3 Colors of Ministry.* St. Charles, IL: Church Smart Resources, 2001.

Silvoso, Ed. *Women: God's Secret Weapon.* Ventura, CA: Regal, 2001.

Towns, Ruth and Elmer. *Women Gifted for Ministry, How to Discover and Practice Your Spiritual Gifts.* Nashville, TN: Thomas Nelson Publishers, 2001.

Wagner, C. Peter. *Your Spiritual Gifts Can Help Your Church Grow.* Ventura, CA: Regal, 1979.

NOTES

CHAPTER 1
THE SIGNIFICANCE OF MOTIVATIONAL GIFTS

1. C. Peter Wagner, *Your Spiritual Gifts Can Help Your Church Grow* (Ventura, CA: Regal Publishing, 1979), 72.
2. Don and Katie Fortune, *Discover Your God-Given Gifts* (Grand Rapids, MI: Chosen Books, 1987), 32.
3. Ibid., 32.

CHAPTER 2
LITTLE IS MUCH WHEN GOD IS IN IT: MARTHA OF BETHANY

1. *NIV Study Bible* (Grand Rapids, MI: Zondervan, 1985), 1618. See note on John 11:17.
2. Peggy Musgrove, *Who's Who Among Bible Women* (Springfield, MO: Gospel Publishing, 1981), 90.
3. Linda Rios Brook, president of Lakeland Leadership League, as heard on a recording.
4. Fortune, *Discover Your God-Given Gifts*, 26.
5. George O. Wood, *A Psalm in Your Heart* (Springfield, MO: Gospel Publishing House, 1997), 77.
6. Tommy Tenney, "We Need Mary and Martha in the House," *SpiritLed Woman* (April/May 2002): 50.

CHAPTER 3
IN HIS TIME: MARY, THE MOTHER OF JESUS

1. Fortune, *Discover Your God-Given Gifts*, 26.
2. Ethelbert W. Bullinger, *A Critical Lexicon and Concordance to the English and Greek New Testament* (Grand Rapids, MI: Zondervan, 1975), 804.
3. Jack Hayford, "Your Season of Ministry, How God Has Ordained Time," *Leadership* (Spring 1996): 45.
4. Ibid.

5. Myles Monroe, *Seasons of Change* (Nassau, Bahamas: Pneuma Life Publishing, 1998), 85.

CHAPTER 4
GO TELL IT ON THE MOUNTAIN: THE SAMARITAN WOMAN

1. Clovis G. Chappell, *Sermons on Biblical Characters* (Manila, Philippines: Christian Literature Crusade, 1993), 53.
2. Fortune, *Discover Your God-Given Gifts*, 26.
3. Rick Joyner, *Shadows of Things to Come* (Nashville, TN: Thomas Nelson Publishers, 2001), 10.
4. Frederick Buechner, *Wishful Thinking: A Seeker's ABC*, Revised and expanded (San Francisco, CA: HarperSanFrancisco, 1993), 21.
5. Wagner, *Your Spiritual Gifts Can Help Your Church Grow*, 157.
6. Oswald Chambers, *My Utmost for His Highest* (Westwood, NJ: Barbour and Company, 1935).

CHAPTER 5
BIND US TOGETHER, LORD, BIND US TOGETHER:
EUODIA AND SYNTYCHE

1. Judy L. Brown, *Women Ministers According to Scriptures* (Kearney, NE: Morris Publishing, 1996), 156–157.
2. Fortune, *Discover Your God-Given Gifts*, 46.

CHAPTER 6
JUMP INTO THE RIVER: LYDIA

1. *NIV Study Bible*, 1678. Commentary on Acts 16:13.
2. Ibid., 1801. Philippians introduction.
3. Ruth and Elmer Towns, *Women Gifted for Ministry, How to Discover and Practice Your Spiritual Gifts* (Nashville, TN: Thomas Nelson Publishers, 2001), 57.
4. *Women's Life Bible* (Nashville, TN: Thomas Nelson Publishers, 2001), 1167.

5. F. F. Bruce, *Paul: Apostle of the Heart Set Free* (Grand Rapids, MI: William B. Eerdmans Publishing Co., 1977), 221.
6. C. Peter Wagner, *Acts of the Holy Spirit: A Modern Commentary on the Book of Acts* (Ventura, CA: Regal Books, 2000), 411.
7. Ibid.

CHAPTER 7
TEACH US YOUR WAYS, O LORD: PRISCILLA

1. Ruth Hoppin, *Priscilla's Letter* (Fort Bragg, CA: Lost Coast Press, 1997), 85.
2. John Chrysostom, "First Homily on the Greeting to Priscilla and Aquila," trans. by Catherine Clark Kroeger. *Priscilla Papers* 5.3 (Summer 1991): 18. Emphasis in the original.
3. Betsy Caram, *Women of the Bible* (Rizal, Philippines: Zion Ministerial Institute, 1997), 99.
4. Marilyn Hickey, *Know Your Ministry* (Denver, CO: Marilyn Hickey Ministries, 1986), 36.
5. Loren Cunningham and David Joel Hamilton, *Why Not Women?* (Seattle, WA: YWAM Publishing, 2000), 25
6. Edith Deen, *Great Women of the Christian Faith* (Westwood, NJ: Barbour and Company, 1959), 143.
7. Ibid., 144.

CHAPTER 8
THANK YOU FOR GIVING TO THE LORD: PHOEBE

1. John Polhill, "Paul and the Romans," *Biblical Illustrator,* Fall 2002, 8.
2. Carol Meyers, general editor, *Women in Scripture* (Grand Rapids, MI: William B. Eerdmans Publishing Co., 2000), 135.
3. Fortune, *Discover Your God-Given Gifts*, 26.

ABOUT THE AUTHOR

L ana Heightley is the founder and president of Women
With A Mission (WWAM), based in Colorado Springs. For
eighteen years Lana has been involved in team missions, developing, training, and equipping women in leadership around
the world. Lana has a passion to see women discover their gifts,
talents, purposes, and destinies, and to see them effectively
released into ministry. She conducts seminars, retreats, and
Bible studies, and has held positions in Algow International
and Africa Village Outreach. She also served on the AD2000
Women's Track Advisory Board. She is a graduate of Wagner
Leadership Institute, where she earned her doctorate diploma
in practical ministry and serves as adjunct faculty. In addition, Lana sits on the board of Christians for Renewal and is
a member of the strategic development team for India Gospel
League NA. Lana is a wife, mother, and grandmother. She and
her husband, John, reside in Colorado Springs.

To contact Lana for speaking or training, write or phone
her at:

Women With A Mission
1275 Log Hollow Point
Colorado Springs, CO 80906
(719) 442-0500
womenwam@aol.com

Be sure to check out her Web site at:
www.womenwam.com